David Grossman is the author of seven novels, two works of journalism, and a previous volume of collected commentary. He lives in Jerusalem.

Also by David Grossman

NOVELS
The Smile of the Lamb
See Under: Love
The Book of Intimate Grammar
The Zigzag Kid
Be My Knife
Someone to Run With
Her Body Knows

NONFICTION
The Yellow Wind
Sleeping on a Wire
Death as a Way of Life

Writing in the Dark

Writing in the Dark

David Grossman

Translated from the Hebrew by Jessica Cohen

Picador

———

Farrar, Straus and Giroux

New York

www.picadorusa.com

Picador® is a U.S. registered trademark and is used by Farrar, Straus and Giroux under license from Pan Books Limited.

For information on Picador Reading Group Guides, please contact Picador. E-mail: readinggroupguides@picadorusa.com

Designed by Jonathan D. Lippincott

Grossman, David.
    Writing in the dark : essays on literature and politics / David
Grossman ; translated from the Hebrew by Jessica Cohen.—1st Picador ed.
        p. cm.
    ISBN 978-0-312-42860-0
    1. Literature and history—Israel. 2. Literature and society—Israel.
3. Israeli literature—History and criticism. 4. Jewish literature—History
and criticism. 5. Arab-Israeli conflict. 6. Holocaust, Jewish (1939–1945)
I. Cohen, Jessica. II. Title.
PJ5010.G76 2009
892.4'46—dc22

                                                        2009017276

First published in the United States by Farrar, Straus and Giroux

First Picador Edition: September 2009

10 9 8 7 6 5 4 3 2 1

Contents

Books That Have Read Me   3

The Desire to Be Gisella   29

Writing in the Dark   59

Individual Language and Mass Language   69

Contemplations on Peace   87

Yitzhak Rabin Memorial Rally   121

Writing in the Dark

Books That Have Read Me

An unforgettable scene in Fellini's film *Roma* depicts the discovery of an ancient catacomb filled with breathtaking murals. But when the murals are exposed to the spotlights of the researchers and camera crew, they fade and quickly vanish.

———

Explaining the process of inspiration, for me, is like trying to explain what occurs in a dream. In both cases we must resort to using words to describe an experience that by nature resists definition. In both cases we can *rationally* analyze the events and consider, for example, the themes and characters that may have influenced the dreamer and the needs that led him to conjure up these particular influences rather than others in his dream. But we will always feel that the essence of the dream, its secret, the unique glimmer of contact between the dreamer and the dream, remains an impenetrable riddle.

I remember what I experienced when I felt I was under the rays of a vast and inspiring literary power—when I read Kafka's *Metamorphosis*, for example, or Yaakov Shabtai's *Past Continuous*, or Thomas Mann's *Joseph and His Brothers*. I have no doubt that some part of me, perhaps my innermost core, seemed to be in the realm of a dream. There was a similar intrinsic logic, and a direct dialogue conducted with the deepest and most veiled contents of my soul, almost without the mediation of consciousness.

When I talk, then, of this or the other author and how he or she touched my life and influenced my writing, I know that it is merely the story I tell myself today, in a waking state, under the spotlights, filtered through the natural sifting process of memory.

———

When I was eight years old, my father suggested that I read Sholem Aleichem's *Adventures of Mottel, the Cantor's Son*. Father himself had been a child in the Galician shtetl of Dynow, just a few miles from Lemberg, otherwise known as Lvov. Like Mottel, he had lost his father at a young age and lived with his brothers and sisters and hardworking widowed mother.

Father, who immigrated to Palestine in 1936, did not talk much about his childhood. Only rarely was the curtain drawn to reveal a strange, enchanting, intangible world, almost like a shadow theater. Then I could see my father as a little boy, sitting in the *cheder* opposite a stern teacher who used to fix broken china during class, binding the pieces together with wire. I could see Father at the age of four, walking home from the *cheder* in the dark, lighting his way with a candle stuck inside half a radish—nature's candlestick. I could see the doctor bringing a precious remedy for my grandfather's ailment as he lay on his deathbed: a paper-thin slice of watermelon. And I could see my father looking out the window.

Father handed me *Adventures of Mottel, the Cantor's Son* (in Y. D. Berkowitz's Hebrew translation), and I read the title of the first chapter while he held the book in his hands—"Today's a Holiday—Weeping Is Forbidden!"—and then the following words: "I bet no one was so delighted with the warm sunny days following Passover as I, Mottel, the son of Peissi the Cantor, and as the neighbor's calf, 'Menie' (as I, Mottel, have named him)."

I did not understand a word of what I read, and yet there was something there. I took the book from my father's hands and climbed up onto the windowsill, my favorite reading place. Outside was Beit Mazmil, where the residents were trying to accustom themselves to the neighborhood's newly ordained Hebrew name, Kiryat Yovel. It was a cluster of apartment buildings whose occupants had made their way from seventy exiles and who argued in seventy languages. The dwellers of the tinshack neighborhood, whom we called *asbestonim*, looked on enviously at those who were lucky enough to get a tiny apartment in one of the buildings. There were young couples who confronted life with determined optimism, and Holocaust survivors who walked the streets like shadows and whom we children feared.

"Together we basked in the first warm sunrays of the first mild after-Passover days; together we breathed in the fragrance of the first tender blades of grass that burst through the newly bared earth; and together we crept out of dark narrow prisons to greet the first sunny spring morning. I, son of Peissi the Cantor, emerged from a cold damp cellar which always smells of sour dough and medicines. And Menie, the neighbor's calf, was released from an even worse odor—a small filthy stall, dark and muddy, with crooked battered walls which let in snow in winter and rain in summer."

"Do you like it?" my father asked. "Read, read, it's just how things were with us." And perhaps because of the expression on his face at that moment, I had a sudden illumination: I realized that for the first time, he was inviting me *over there*, giving me the keys to the tunnel that would lead from my childhood to his.

———

It was a peculiar tunnel. One end was in Jerusalem, in the young State of Israel, which believed that its strength depended partly on its ability to forget so that it could cobble together a new identity for itself. And the other end was in the land of Over There.

From the moment I stepped into that land I could not leave. I was eight, and within a few months I had devoured all of Sholem Aleichem's writings that existed in

Hebrew at the time—the children's stories, the writings for adults, and the plays. When I reread the works before writing this piece, I was amazed to discover how little I could have understood as a child, and how powerfully the things beyond the visible text must have worked on me. Because what could an eight- or nine-year-old have understood about Rachel's tormented love for Stempenyu? Or the political views that Sholem Aleichem gave to a detached and wayward Jewish character like Menachem Mendel, or to his complete opposite, Tevye the Milkman? What did I know about the life of yeshiva students who ate at the table of a different homeowner each day of the week? About the hostility between the "landlord" class and the workers, or about the conflict between the Zionists and the Bundists?

I did not know, I did not understand, but something inside me would not allow me to let go of the inscrutable stories, written in a Hebrew I had never encountered before. I read like someone entering a completely foreign world that was, at the same time, a promised land. In some sense, I felt that I was coming home. And it all worked its magic on me in a muddled way: the words with the biblical ring, the characters, the customs, the ways of life, and the fact that the page numbers were marked with letters rather than numbers, as in Bialik and Rawnitzky's *Book of Legends*. Even the smell of the pages was dense and so different from the scent of the other books I read—translations of *The Famous Five* and *The Secret Seven*, *The Paul Street Boys* and *Kajtuś the Wizard*, the works of Erich Kestner and Jules Verne, and

Israeli books like Shraga Gafni's adventure stories, Eliezer Smoli's *Frontiersmen of Israel*, the adventures of the secret agent named Oz Yaoz, books by Nachum Gutman, and anything else I could get my hands on.

Parenthetically I will add that I belong to a generation that was accustomed to reading texts in which they did not understand every single word. In the early 1960s we read books in archaic and poetic Hebrew; we read translations from the 1920s and '30s that did not employ our daily language at all. The incomprehensibility imposed on us was certainly a barrier to fluid reading, but in hindsight I think that part of my reading experience in that period came from this very same incomprehensibility: the mystery and the exoticism of words with an odd ring, and the pleasure of inferring one thing from another. I note this because most children's books today (and children's magazines even more so) are written at the readers' eye level and ear level, if not lower, usually preferring the simplest—and sometimes the most simplistic—words possible, often favoring slang. Of course this has many advantages and perhaps results in a broader readership, yet I miss the reading experience of my own childhood, when in the course of reading, the child would fill in linguistic gaps and unwittingly acquire a large and rich vocabulary, learning to view language as an entity with a life of its own.

————

Inside the six volumes of Sholem Aleichem—a collection of small red books published by Dvir—I discovered the

most imaginative world I had ever found in any book. It
was a world that was neither heroic nor grand, ostensibly
containing nothing that could draw the heart of a child.
But it spoke to me, and must have given voice to a longing, a real hunger, that I had not even imagined before. I
read about cunning matchmakers, tailors, and water-
drawers; about tutors (*melamdim*) and pupils (*dardakim*)
in the *cheder*; about priests and laundresses and snuff-
takers and smugglers. I read about sheepskin mantles
and peasant overcoats. I met moneylenders and usurers,
and robbers who attack you in the woods at night. There
were places called Kasrilevke and Yehupitz, and people
called Hersh Leib, Shneyer, Menachem Mendel, Ivan
Pichkur, and Father Alexei. Strangest of all was that Jews
lived together with *goyim*. What did this mean? Why did
they want to live with these dangerous *goyim*? Why did
Tevye's daughter Chavaleh marry a *goy*? And why did the
goyim throw Tevye out of his home, and how was it possible so simply, with the wave of an arm, to uproot a man
from his home and his life and tell him, "Go"?

Incidentally, I did not fully comprehend the meaning
of the word *goy*, and the term "Christian" was also a little
vague. I am fairly certain that until the age of nine I was
positive—perhaps like many children—that "Christian"
(in Hebrew, *notzri*) was a type of Egyptian (in Hebrew,
mitzri). Either way, they were both "the enemy."

———

Everything in the stories amazed and daunted and at-
tracted me: the sense of a tenuous existence; the suf-

fering embedded in the everyday; the constant fear of
pogroms or "hunts"; the fluent dialogue with God, almost like small talk; and the absolute authority of dreams
and their meanings. There was also the constant presence of the dead, a series of "patriarchs" and "matri-
archs" with whom people conversed on a daily basis even
if they had been dead for years. And the experience of
total dependence on despots, the fatalism, the physical
weakness, the compassion—even toward those who hate
you—and the irony, and again and again the peculiar intimacy with calamity, the calamity that always hovered
over everyone's head so that its imminence was never in
doubt.

It is worth noting that I did not know any other children who read Sholem Aleichem. When I excitedly told
my best friend in the neighborhood about my new experience, he gave me a sideways look and his lips began to
curl into a smirk. I quickly changed the subject, but the
incident forced me to make increased efforts in such
pursuits as suicidal leaps from trees and climbing up tall
cranes, all to clear my briefly sullied name. Very quickly,
with a child's instinct—a survivor's instinct—I realized
that the shtetl must remain my secret world, to be shared
with no one.

———

Between the ages of eight and ten I was a double agent
from "here" to Over There and back again. I conducted
an intensive life in both realities, experiencing with great

enthusiasm all that life in Israel of the early 1960s had to offer—a spirited existence that was both miserable and miraculous. Like most children in the neighborhood, I worked tirelessly to expose Arab spies (half the country was busy with that) and spent days in physical training so that I could either make it onto the Israeli team that would defeat the evil Germans or get into the paratroopers. But whenever possible I dived back into my Jewish shtetl, which was becoming more and more tangible, comprehensible, and relevant to me, animating within me some Jewish note—that was at the same time very diasporic—giving it a voice and sensations, and a clear existence in my world.

———

The odd thing was that all that time I was convinced that the world of Sholem Aleichem—the world of the Eastern European shtetl—continued to exist alongside my own. Not that I dwelled much on the question of its existence or lack thereof in reality: its literary form was so bold and vital that it never even occurred to me to ponder its subsistence outside the pages of the six volumes. But in the recesses of my mind it was clear to me that this world did indeed live on somewhere out there, with its various laws and institutions, its special language, and its mystery. It was a world always accompanied by a sad yet smiling melody, a lamentation resigned to the loss— but the loss of what? That I did not know.

And then when I was about nine and a half, in the

midst of a Holocaust Remembrance Day ceremony, one
of those clumsy, hackneyed, repetitive rituals that are so
helpless in the face of the thing itself, in the face of that
unfathomable number, six million . . .

It struck me all at once. Suddenly. The six million, the
murdered, the victims, the "Holocaust martyrs," all those
terms were in fact *my* people. They were Mottel and
Tevye and Shimele Soroker and Chavaleh and Stem
penyu and Lily and Shimek. On the burning asphalt of
the Beit Hakerem school, the shtetl was suddenly taken
from me.

It was the first time I truly understood the meaning
of the Holocaust. And it is no exaggeration to say that
this comprehension shook my entire world. I remember
my distress during the following days, a distress charac-
teristic of the children of real survivors, because I imagined that I now bore some responsibility to remember all
those people; it was a responsibility I did not want.

Every child has his first experience of death. The
characters in Sholem Aleichem's stories were the first
people to die in my life. I could not read about them any
longer, yet I could not stop reading. For a while I read in
a way I never had: with care and gravity, I read all six volumes again, for the last time (I was very careful not to
laugh in the places that always made me laugh), and the
reading was both my contact with the intolerable pain
and my only way to heal it. Each encounter with the text
brought home to me again the enormity of the loss, but
somehow also made it a little more tolerable. Today I
know that at ten I discovered that books are the place in

the world where both the thing and the loss of it can co-exist.

————

The first part of *See Under: Love* tells of a boy named Momik who tries to understand the Diaspora in Israeli terms. Large parts of the book are an attempt to write about a *Jewish* existence in an *Israeli* idiom. But it also attempts the opposite: to describe Israel in a "diasporic" language. That is the book's internal music, its counter-point.

See Under: Love is a novel about a story that was lost, torn to shreds. There are several such lost stories in the book, which have to be told again and again because that is the only way to assemble the traces of identity and fuse the fragments of a crumbled world. Many characters in the book are looking for a story they have lost, usually a childhood tale, and they need it very badly so that they can retell it, as adults, and be reborn through it. It is not innocence that drives their desire to tell children's sto-ries, for they have virtually no innocence left. Rather, this is their way to preserve their humanity, and perhaps a modicum of nobility—to believe in the possibility of child-hood in this world, and to hold it up against the sheer cynicism. To tell the whole story again through the eyes of a child.

————

The arbitrariness of an external force that violently in-vades the life of one person, one soul, preoccupies me in almost all my books. In *See Under: Love* it was Nazism; in *The Smile of the Lamb* and *The Yellow Wind* it was a military occupation that views itself as enlightened, while its victims are subjected to the tyranny of a power they perceive as supreme; in *The Book of Intimate Grammar* I tried to describe the way one's soul—that multifarious glimmer of life—is forced to adapt to the impersonal dimensions of matter, to the unequivocal quality of flesh.

From one book to the next I found that if I could be more precise in describing the relationship between the individual soul and this external arbitrariness, if I struggled a little harder with the depth of descriptions, the subtlety of sensations, the nuances of "being there," I could conquer another millimeter of the void between myself and what had always seemed unalterable. Not that I found a better way to live in peace with the contradictions between body and mind; not that I truly understood how a man can erase himself to such a degree that he becomes part of a destructive machine; and not that if I were to describe the injustices of the Occupation it would be over. But my inner stance vis-à-vis the unalterable shifted slightly: I could give my own private names and definitions to states that had seemed frozen, eternal, monolithic, decreed from above or from below. I was no longer a victim of the things that had theretofore paralyzed me with fear and despair.

This feeling brings me to another precious source of inspiration and awe—the writing of Bruno Schulz. I first heard about *The Street of Crocodiles* (originally titled

Cinnamon Shops) from a stranger who phoned me one
day after reading *The Smile of the Lamb* to tell me,
warmly but firmly, that I was of course deeply influenced
by Bruno Schulz. As I said, I did not know Schulz's work
at the time, and I was happy to learn how much he had
influenced me. In fact, I have frequently been informed
by my erudite critics about certain writers who have influenced me, and after reading them for the first time, I
have discovered that the critics were correct.

Bruno Schulz, a Polish Jewish writer who lived in the
town of Drohobycz, also in Galicia, was a modest art
teacher who turned his small domestic life into a tremen-
dous mythology, and today he is considered one of the
greatest writers of the twentieth century. Bruno Schulz
believed and hoped that our daily life was but a series
of legendary episodes, fragments of ancient carved im-
ages, crumbs of shattered mythologies. He likened human language to a primeval snake that was long ago
cut into a thousand pieces—these pieces are the words
that have ostensibly lost their primeval vitality and now
function solely as a means of communication, yet still, always, they continue "to search for one another in the
dark."

On every page written by Bruno Schulz one can feel
this restless search, the longing for a different, primordial wholeness. His stories are full of the moments of
first contact, when words suddenly "find one another in
the dark." That is when an electric spark of sorts occurs
in the reader's consciousness, awakening the sense that a

word he or she has heard and read a thousand times can now momentarily reveal its private name.

Only two collections of Schulz's short stories have been published, as well as a few other shorter works. He wrote a novel titled *The Messiah*, which was lost, and no one knows for certain what it contained. I once met a man who told me that Schulz had shown him the first few lines of the novel: Morning rises above a town A certain light. Towers. That was all he saw.

Although Schulz did not write much, life bursts forth from every page he did produce, overflowing, becoming worthy of its name, a colossal effort that occurs simultaneously on all levels of consciousness and unconsciousness, illusion and nostalgia and nightmare. I read the book over the course of one day and night in a total frenzy of the senses, and my feeling—which now slightly embarrasses me—will be familiar to anyone who has been in love: it was the knowledge that this other person or thing was meant only for me.

I read the entire book (*Cinnamon Shops & Sanatorium Under the Sign of the Hourglass*, published in Hebrew by Schocken) without knowing a thing about Bruno Schulz, and when I reached the end, I read Yoram Bronowski's afterword, where I learned the story of Schulz's death. In the Drohobycz ghetto, Schulz had a protector and employer in the form of an S.S. officer named Landau, who had Schulz paint murals in his home and stable. The officer had a rival, another S.S. officer named Günter, who lost a card game to Landau. Günter met

Bruno Schulz on a street corner and shot him dead to hurt his employer. When the two officers later met, the murderer said: "I killed your Jew." To which the other responded: "Very well. Now I will kill your Jew."

———

After reading this account, I felt that I did not wish to live in a world in which such monstrosities of language could be uttered. But this time, unlike my paralysis at age ten— after realizing the connection between the horrors of the Holocaust and the characters of Sholem Aleichem—I had a way to express what I felt. I wanted to write a book that would tell readers about Bruno Schulz. It would be a book that would tremble on the shelf. The vitality it contained would be tantamount to the blink of an eye in one person's life—not "life" in quotation marks, life that is nothing more than a languishing moment in time, but the sort of life Schulz gives us in his writing. A life of the living.

I know that many readers of *See Under: Love* found it difficult to get through the chapter on Bruno Schulz. But for me, that is the core of the book, the reason I wrote it, the reason I write. When people tell me they were unable to read it, I am regretful over the missed encounter, which is why the meetings I have had with those who were willing to delve into that chapter with me are so precious. The book has since been translated into several languages, and nothing makes me happier than the fact that in each language in which the book has appeared,

new editions of Bruno Schulz's writings have soon followed, and more and more people have become ac-
quainted with this wonderful writer.

———

When I was invited to write about my sources of inspiration, I was asked which books I would like to discuss and
what should be included in the bibliography for students.
I began to think about which books and writers have influenced me and shaped my writing, and there have
been so many: the stories of A. B. Yehoshua, Amos
Oz's *Hill of Evil Counsel*, Kafka's works, Thomas Mann's
Magic Mountain, Heinrich Böll, Virginia Woolf, and
many others. Of course I was tempted to lecture about
Joyce and Camus, of whom I am particularly fond, and to
frustrate some of the distinguished scholars with quota-
tions from a Greenlandic epic they have never heard of.

But when Bialik wrote his poem "My Song," he did
not speak of his *literary* sources of inspiration. That was
not the poem in which he described the bookshelves he
stood facing as a boy, and later left behind. "Do you
know whence I derived my song?" he asks. And he
replies by recalling the dry, empty voice of a cricket that
lived in his father's house, and his mother's deep sigh
when she was widowed.

A cricket, a sigh.

And so I will not speak of authors or books that in-
spired me, but of an almost physical sensation that may
not be a source of inspiration in the traditional sense, yet

I feel it is a distinct root of my need to write. I find it difficult to reduce this sensation to a verbal definition. Bruno Schulz talks of suffocation within "the fortressed walls of tedium that close in on us"; perhaps it is that suffocation. Perhaps it is a type of claustrophobia that arises within the words of others. To understand it, I wrote a whole book, *The Book of Intimate Grammar*, which is the story of a young man who cannot accept the burden of all the conventions and routines that surround him, or the verbal clichés, or even the restrictive, unequivocal, physical dictates of his own body.

———

The book takes place in 1960s Jerusalem. Aron Kleinfeld lives in what is essentially a society of refugees, filled with people who have recently escaped a catastrophe and are trying with their last remaining strength to create a new life, a new language. With sometimes grotesque fervor, they grasp onto objects, food, anything with tangible volume. They create a solid, corporeal, unequivocal world, and it is naturally a world that is extremely belligerent and arbitrary, recklessly invading the privacy of its individuals.

To me, it is a book about the birth of an artist from within those "fortressed walls of tedium." Aron, who is twelve when the story begins, a bright and imaginative child with abundant happiness, feels this invasion increasingly stifling him. It is all around him, shoving rude fingers into his mind and body. Even the physiological process of maturation that he faces seems to be a part of it. (Incidentally, the Hebrew words for "muscle"—*shrir*—and "arbitrariness"—*shrirut*—come from the same root.)

Alienation and, ultimately, hostility emerge between Aron and his own flesh and body—between himself and the part of his being that has an external, objective, yet extremely internal existence. Aron sees his friends begin to mature and change, as if collectively obeying an invisible order, and he is incapable of joining them. There is something in the unity of the process, in its inevitability, that deters him because he finds it lacking in freedom, almost humiliating.

Aron's case is of course an extreme one, but I imagine we all remember the feelings of our adolescence, when we entered a tunnel that would stretch out for a number of years without knowing what fate had in store for us, how we would emerge at the other end, woven into which body, woven into which soul. As the years go by, we come to know the thing that Aron feared most, unknowingly of course, and which probably made him refuse to accept this constitution of the flesh: the knowledge of how easy it is for the mind to surrender to the corporeal dimension and gradually become a mechanism much like that of the body—with clogged arteries, cramped muscles, rigid joints, and automatic reflexes.

Faced with the bureaucracy of the body imposed on him, Aron feels that the primary means through which he can express his freedom, his uniqueness, and even his sexuality is language. And since language is also a kind of body, with a dual existence, both inside and out, Aron is tormented every time there is a grating contact between that "inside" and that "outside": when people around him use language like old saws, when they belittle something that in Aron's soul has a different, purer, more loyal existence. From that particular moment he realizes instinctively that he can no longer use words as others do—indiscriminately, indifferently, inarticulately.

———

It is also relevant to note that the story occurs shortly before the Six-Day War, when everyone Aron meets talks in the same blunt, military style, born of fear and arrogance. They all prophesize in the same tone, and this depresses Aron to no end, both because of the crudeness that characterizes the uniform, slogan-ridden discourse and because of his sense that they all belong to a secret, hermetic system of symbols from which he himself is removed, and that he will never have the requisite crudeness or obtuseness to become a part of it.

Deep within himself, beneath his heart, Aron establishes a hospital for sick words, where he employs complex rituals to heal and purify the words he gathers from the day-to-day. Only when the purification process is complete does he feel entitled to use the words. They have passed through his body and soul. They are his. Of course this process condemns Aron to utter solitude, trapped in his inner world, in his own private language, creating his beloved and his best friend inside himself, unable to maintain normal relationships with them in what is termed "reality." The book ends when Aron shuts himself up inside an old refrigerator and hopes that with the help of the childlike, artistic spark he used to have, he will be able to pull off his most difficult Houdini trick and break out of the refrigerator into the world. But will he in fact be able to?

I have my own answer to this question, but before I reach it I would like to shift from the private, personal language to the more general kind, which served as a sort of "inspiration in reverse" for three of my books: the novel *The Smile of the Lamb* and two works of nonfiction, *The Yellow Wind* and *Sleeping on a Wire*. Each of these books, in its own way, tries to describe contemporary political reality in a language that is not the public, general, nationalized idiom.

———

To our great misfortune, we in Israel have been living for almost a century in a state of violent conflict, which has an enormous influence on all realms of life, including, of course, on language. When a country or a society finds itself—no matter for what reasons—in a prolonged state of incongruity between its founding values and its political circumstances, a rift can emerge between the society and its identity, between the society and its "inner voice." The more complex and contradictory the situation becomes and the more the society has to compromise in order to contain all its disparities, the more it creates a different system for itself, an ad hoc system of norms, of "emergency values," keeping double books of its identity.

I am not saying anything new here. Those who live in such a reality, as we do in Israel, will find it easy to understand how fears consolidate ideals around themselves, how needs become values, and how a subjective worldview and a self-image that is wholly unsuited to reality can materialize. A special kind of language then begins to emerge, one that is usually a manipulation on the part of those who wish to prolong the distorted situation. It is a language of words intended not to describe reality but to obfuscate it, to allay it. It depicts a reality that does not exist, an imaginary state constructed by wishful thinking, while large and complex elements of the actual reality remain wordless, in the hope that they will somehow fade away and vanish. In such conditions one of our most dubious talents arises: the talent for passivity, for self-erasure, for reducing the inner surface of our soul lest it get hurt. In other words, the talent for being a victim.

Let us go back eleven years, to the spring of 1987.

For two decades, as a result of the Six-Day War, Israel has controlled more than two million Palestinians. By all opinions this is a grave state of affairs, yet it turns out that most Israelis, as well as most Palestinians, have taught themselves how to live in these warped circumstances and that many of them believe the situation will never change. As time goes by, there is an increasing per-

ception of a "status quo," along with more and more arguments that justify and even sanctify this very status
quo. The press provides scarcely any news of what is going on in the Territories, only brief reports of violent in-
cidents phrased in fixed formulas that are little more
than slogans and do not catch one's eye for very long.

At this time I was working as a newscaster on the Kol
Israel radio news. I was given dozens, if not hundreds, of
items to read that sounded something like this: "A local
youth was killed during disturbances in the Territories."
Notice the shrewdness of the sentence: "disturbances"—
as if there were some order or normative state in the
Territories that was briefly disturbed; "in the Territories"—we would never expressly say "the Occupied
Territories"; "youth"—this youth might have been a
three-year-old boy, and of course he never had a name;
"local"—so as not to say "Palestinian," which would imply someone with a clear national identity; and above all,
note the verb "was killed"—no one killed him. It would
have been almost intolerable to admit that our hands
spilled this blood, and so he "was killed." (Sometimes the
passive voice is the last refuge of the patriot.)

Because we lost the capacity to use the right words to
describe reality, we woke up one day, in December 1987,
to a reality that is difficult to describe. Israel had de-
ceived itself so efficiently that the Israel Defense Forces
did not even have contingency plans to deal with the
mass protests. At the beginning of the intifada the security apparatus dispatched urgent envoys to the world's

most dubious markets to purchase rubber bullets, gravel-spraying vehicles, and other necessities. Yet any country that occupies and oppresses another people must be prepared for such large-scale demonstrations. Israel was not prepared, because it did not know it was an occupier, it did not think it was an oppressor, and it did not tell itself that there was a people out there.

———

Nine months before the intifada broke out, I wrote *The Yellow Wind*. The book presented nothing new in the way of facts, which had been exposed ad nauseam. But in order to truly understand what I was seeing and feeling, I had to articulate the facts with new words. And from the moment I started writing, from the day I went to the Dheisheh refugee camp and encountered a reality that until that time I had lacked the words to describe, I felt something I had not felt for years, certainly not in the political context: that consciousness, in any situation, is always free to choose to face reality in a different, new way. That writing about reality is the simplest way to not be a victim.

In this sense, writing the nonfiction books made me feel that I was reclaiming parts of myself that the prolonged conflict had expropriated or turned into "closed military zones." Furthermore, I came to grasp the high price we were paying for willingly giving up on parts of our soul—a price no less painful than giving up land. I knew that we were not killing only the Palestinians, and I

asked why we were continuing to accept not just the
murder, but the suicide too.

————

The name of the novel *Be My Knife* is a paraphrase of a
line Franz Kafka wrote to Milena: "Love is to me that
you are the knife which I turn within myself." *The Book
of Intimate Grammar* could not have been written without *See Under: Love*, which preceded it; *Be My Knife*
could not have been written without *The Book of Intimate Grammar*; and *Be My Knife*, in turn, was probably
the basis for the book that followed it. It is clear to me
now that this is a very long path, which must be followed
slowly, and that I must recognize that an entire lifetime
will not suffice to map out even the first bend in the
path.

In *The Book of Intimate Grammar*, I articulated several complicated ideas that I needed to understand, in
sentences that today cover the pages in front of me like a
verdict. But they are precisely what enabled me to find
the strength to step out of Aron Kleinfeld's loneliness, to
escape from the refrigerator at the end of that book and
start walking—this time in a different literary situation,
with a different, more mature literary character—toward
a different person. This would no longer be the imaginary creation of my protagonist, but a man who lives in
reality and a woman of flesh and blood. I had to believe
that it is possible for a different person to occur within
myself, to believe without fear that a person can dwell

inside the body and soul and language of another. And to discover that one can find a partner to share the deepest and most silent anxieties, and keys to unlock the most despicable self-laid traps.

Be My Knife is also the story of a journey to find the right language. A journey in which the woman is a tour guide of sorts who leads the man to his real language, which she carves out of him in a difficult battle until, near the end of the book, they create their own language. The book tries to be the only place where there can be a meaning for this private language—the language of their love.

This essay was written in 1998, and was first published in 2002.

The Desire to Be Gisella

If asked to describe the qualities that motivate someone to become an author, the first I'd name would be a strong urge to invent stories: to organize reality, which is frequently chaotic and unintelligible, within a structure of storytelling; to find the visible and hidden contexts that load every event with its particular meaning; to accentuate the shades of "plot" within each such event and coax out its "heroes."

To me, the urge to tell a story, whether invented or rendered from reality, is almost an instinct: the storytelling instinct. In some people—a number of whom eventually become writers—it is as powerful and primal as any other instinct. Fortunately, it always encounters its counterpart: the instinct to listen to stories.

There is something moving about people's need to listen to a story. Sometimes I sit on a stage and read to an audience. These readings usually take place in the evening, when the members of the audience, most of whom are not very young, have come from a full day of work, and their lives are not always easy. But when I look up from the page from time to time, I see before me a wonderful sight: within a matter of moments, it is as if these people's faces have shed the tiredness, the difficulties, the sadness, and sometimes the bitterness, grumbling, and anxieties, and something soft and forgotten comes over their faces. For a moment one can feel—even see—how they used to be as children.

(Perhaps this is the thing: there is something childlike—not childish, but childlike, primal—in the storytelling urge, and no less so in the urge to *hear* a story.)

Other qualities that might make one become a writer include a desire to explain, through story, the world and the human beings who inhabit it, with all their differences, their travails, and their reversals. One could also add the writer's desire to know himself, to express all the currents that flow inside him. A person who does not have these desires and primal urges is unlikely to be able—if he is even willing—to invest the vast emotional efforts that writing demands.

———

But today I would like to talk of a different motive for writing, one that is undoubtedly related in some way to those I have just mentioned. It grows stronger within me as I age—both in life years and in writing years—and as I experience an increasing need for the act of creation and writing as a way of life, as a way of finding my place in the world.

The motive I am referring to is the wish to strip away

what protects me from the Other. To remove the usually invisible barrier that separates me from any other person. The desire to expose myself completely, without any defenses, to the individuality and life of another person, to his most elemental inner workings, in their unprocessed, primordial form.

But these wishes are immediately faced with a great obstacle, because the more I examine myself and observe human beings in general, near and far, the more I reach a conclusion that at first surprises and disappoints me, and so I quickly dismiss it as a baseless generalization. Yet it sneaks back again and again, in countless examples and variations, and so I will say it, and you may utterly discount it and determine that it holds not a shred of truth.

My conclusion is that in many ways, we humans—social creatures known for our warmth and empathy toward our families, friends, and communities—are not only efficiently protected and fortressed against our enemies, but in some ways also protected—meaning, we protect ourselves—*from any Other*. From the projection of the Other's internality onto ourselves; from the way this internality is demandingly and constantly thrown at us; from something that I will call "the chaos within the Other."

"Hell is other people," said Sartre, and perhaps our fear of the hell that exists in others is the reason that the paper-thin layer of skin that envelops us and separates us from others is sometimes as impervious as any fortified wall or border.

If we observe those around us, we will find that even between couples who have lived together for decades— who have lived more or less happily, and who love each other and function well as parents and as a family—there can often be, almost instinctively and unwittingly, a complex unspoken agreement (whose application, incidentally, requires a most sophisticated and nuanced form of collaboration!), the main tenet of which is that it is best not to know one's partner through and through. Not to be exposed to all that happens within him. And not to recognize these "occurrences" or name them explicitly, because they have no place within the framework of the couple's relationship, and they might even tear the relationship apart from the inside and bring it crashing down, something neither partner desires.

("It is only now so clear to me," writes one man, in one book—*Be My Knife*, a novel with which I had a complicated couplehood—"that my life with my wife, our love, is so stable and defined that it is impossible to add a new element that is too large, like myself, for instance.")

Sometimes I look at a couple that has been together for a long time—there are quite a few whom I know; you may have come across some too—and I perform a little exercise of thought and imagination: I try to see what they were like at the moment they were created as a couple. I try to remove all the layers of time and age and weariness and routine, and then I can see them young and fresh, and so innocent. Sometimes I can also observe how, at the moment of their "pollination" as a couple,

they seemed to conduct a silent dialogue, like one subconscious talking to another, in which they promptly
agreed on the angles in which they would view each
other for the rest of their lives, thus instantly entering a
complicated life pact, wondrous in its complexity and
subtle mechanisms. They may also have determined that
their love would always win, at any cost. Because there is
always a price to pay for not seeing the person closest to
us from all possible angles, not seeing all his sides and all
his shadows. There is a price to pay when we animate in
our partner—and when our partner animates in himself—only certain "areas of the soul," which are defined
and agreed upon, and therefore restricted.

A similar process occurs, of course, between parents
and children. Sometimes, especially when we are very
young, it is not easy for us to see our parents from a
broad angle. It may also be uncomfortable for us to accept that our parents are "entitled" to their own internal
chaos. That Mom and Dad too have not only souls but
also—horror of horrors!—a right to their own "psychol-
ogy." And that they too had mothers and fathers, and that
those parents, in their day, did things that left wounds
and scars and aberrations in our parents.

Perhaps the most difficult thing is to expose ourselves
to the darkness we often sense in our children, particularly when they are young and tender. It is difficult to admit to ourselves that even in those delicate, innocent
souls there may be a dark chasm, whence threatening
desires and urges and foreignness and madness may

erupt. As a parent, I can attest that even the thought of this is intolerable, perhaps chiefly because of the guilt it arouses.

We can also find this sort of demarcation between friends, even "best friends" or true soul mates. Even in the deepest, longest, and most loyal friendships, a thin barrier is sometimes detectable—a refusal to know everything, a form of protection, transparent but solid, from that unseen darkness within our best friend.

I recall the tragicomic dialogue between Vladimir and Estragon in *Waiting for Godot*. "I had a dream," says Estragon. "Don't tell me!" Vladimir immediately retorts. "Who am I to tell my private nightmares to if I can't tell them to you?" Estragon asks. "Let them remain private," replies Vladimir.

On second thought, perhaps the unwillingness—the fear?—to be exposed to the complexities of people close to us should not be so surprising, for experience teaches us that people are rarely eager to be truly exposed even to what exists *within themselves*. Perhaps our attempt to avoid being fully exposed to the Other is not so different from the efforts we make—almost inadvertently—to resist being tempted by all the varied "others" within each of us. To keep from crumbling into all the options of existence and the internal temptations, all the forking paths within us. Who can measure the vast efforts we make to maintain these rigid internal frameworks, to preserve the bands that grasp—and sometimes shackle—our many-faceted, oft-deceptive souls?

I will add that I often feel that writing has shown me the enormous effort I continually make, often unconsciously, to resist falling apart into all the possibilities, all the many characters and entities, all the qualities and urges and instincts that act within me, well suppressed yet still pulling me constantly in all directions.

———

We human beings are uneasy about what truly occurs deep inside the Other, even if that Other is someone we love. And perhaps it is more than unease; perhaps it is an actual fear of the mysterious, nonverbal, unprocessed core, that which cannot be subjected to any social taming, to any refinement, politeness, or tact; that which is instinctive, wild, and chaotic, not at all politically correct. It is dreamlike and nightmarish, radical and exposed, sexual and unbridled, at least according to the social-order definitions that prevail among "civilized" people (whatever that term may mean). It is mad and sometimes cruel, often animalistic, for good or for bad. It is, if you will, the magma, the primordial, blazing material that bubbles inside every person simply because he is human, simply because he is an intersection of so many forces, instincts, longings, and urges. It is a magma that usually, among sane people—even the most tempestuous—hardens and cools when it comes into contact with air, when it encounters other human beings, or the confines of reality, and then it becomes part of "normative" social fiber.

To me, writing, the writing of literature, is partly an

act of protest and defiance, and even *rebellion*, against this fear—against the temptation to entrench myself, to set up an almost imperceptible barrier, one that is friendly and courteous but very effective, between myself and others, and ultimately between me and myself.

I wish to clarify again that the primary urge that motivates and engenders writing, in my view, is the writer's desire to invent and tell a story, and to know *himself*. But the more I write, the more I feel the force of the other urge, which collaborates with and completes the first one: the desire *to know the Other from within him*. To feel what it means to be another person. To be able to touch, if only for a moment, the blaze that burns within another human being.

This may be something we cannot achieve by any other means. We tend to think that when we merge completely with another person, in moments of love and sexual contact, we know that person in an incomparable way. In biblical Hebrew the sexual act is even connoted with the verb "to know": "And the man knew Eve his wife," says Genesis. But at the highest moments of love, if we are not completely focused, on ourselves or on a pointed projection of our heart's desires onto our partner, we are usually directed mainly toward what is good, beautiful, attractive, and sweet in him. Not to all his complexities, all his different tones and shades—in short, not to everything that makes him "an Other" in the deepest and fullest sense of the word. But when we *write* about the Other, about any Other, we aspire to reach the knowledge that encompasses the unloved parts in him as well, the parts that deter and threaten. The places where his soul is shattered and his consciousness crumbles. The bubbling cauldron of extremism and sexuality and animalism that I mentioned previously. The fount of magma, before it has hardened, and long before it has turned into words.

Even if, almost inevitably, we "project" our soul onto the Other we are writing about, and even if we often "use" the Other to tell stories about ourselves and to understand ourselves, still the *wish* that I am speaking of, in its purest essence, aspires precisely in the opposite direction: to boldly cast off the shackles of my "I" and reach the core of the Other, as an Other, and to then experience the Other *as one who exists to himself and for himself*, as a whole world with its own validity and internal logic. It is then that we are able to catch a glimpse of—and even linger in—the place that is usually so difficult and rare to know in another. The place where we are exposed to the Other's "core," where dreams and nightmares, hallucinations, terrors, and yearnings are created—all the things that make us human.

What is interesting to discover is that at those rare moments when I manage to make this wish come true and reach that "core" of the Other, it is then that I—the writer—do not have a sense of losing myself, or of being assimilated into this particular Other about whom I have written, but rather I have a more lucid perception of "the otherness of the Other," of the differentiation of this

Other from myself. There is a sharp and mature sense of
something I might call "the principle of Otherness."

I further believe that when we read a book that was
written this way, in which the author reached that
sought-after place and was able to know the Other from
within him but still remain himself, we readers experience a unique sensation of spiritual elevation, of sharing
a rare opportunity to touch a precious human secret, a
deep existential experience. This sensation is accompanied by another, no less precious and moving, which is a
true intimacy with the person about whom the story is
told. It is a sense of deep, empathetic understanding of
the character and his motives, even if we utterly disagree
with them. At these times we catch sight of a similarity—
sometimes surprising, sometimes enraging and threatening—between this character and ourselves. And thus,
even if the character arouses resistance, aversion, or dis-
gust, these reactions no longer create in us a total alienation to the character; they do not separate us from him.
They prevent us from sharply, unequivocally, perhaps
uncompassionately condemning the character. On the
contrary: we often feel that only by some miraculous
twist of fate have we been spared from becoming that
detestable character ourselves, and that the possibility of
being that character still exists and murmurs within us, in
our genetic reservoir.

———

We must not only embody the *soul* of the Other when we
write of him but also be under his skin, inside his body,

experiencing his limitations and flaws, his beauty and ugliness. In this context, I would like to recall a little story.

A few years ago, my book *See Under: Love* was published. Some weeks later, I was taking an evening bus from Tel Aviv to Jerusalem, listening to the news hour on the radio along with the other passengers. In the "cultural segment" of the program (culture, as we know, should always be confined to a segment, so that it does not swell and seep into the more important news), a stage actor read an excerpt from my novel. The passage described Gisella, Momik's mother, sitting at her sewing machine, a well-known Singer model, her foot moving up and down on some sort of pedal that Uncle Shimmik had installed for her at the bottom of the machine.

At that moment, the bus driver, who apparently could no longer tolerate the story's gloom and doom, turned the radio dial and switched us all to a more upbeat channel playing Israeli music. I imagine most of the passengers breathed a sigh of relief, but I was left distraught, because of the private insult—mine and my book's—but also because I could not understand which pedal the excerpt was referring to, and why on earth Uncle Shimmik had installed an extra pedal. The Singer I remembered had its own perfectly comfortable metal treadle, and I am not in the habit of throwing accessories or instruments into my stories for no reason. I could not comprehend what had made me add this device when I wrote the book.

I was on edge for the rest of the journey. When I finally got home, I quickly opened the book and found the excerpt. Indeed, shortly after the point at which the bus driver had cut the segment off, I found out that Gisella's foot simply did not reach the original Singer treadle. In another part of the book, I learned something that had somehow escaped my memory: Gisella was an extremely short woman.

I remember being filled with happiness, because I had suddenly discovered something simple and profound about writing. If I had a broken blind at home, for example, or a door handle that needed fixing, it would undoubtedly take weeks before I found the time to repair it. My wife would have to remind me every few days, I would leave myself notes in all sorts of places (and promptly forget about them), and finally, when I no longer had any choice and the family members' protests were jeopardizing my already rather tenuous standing as head of the household, I would give in and fix it. But when I write a story and a short and stocky woman named Gisella walks around in this story, then, when I write her, *I become Gisella*. Even if she is a marginal character, even if she only passes through for a few pages, I must, I want, I long to be Gisella. And when I write Gisella, I walk like Gisella and eat like Gisella and toss and turn in my sleep like Gisella. I run after buses heavily, like her, and I measure every walking distance by the steps of her short, thick, bandaged feet. And when I sit my Gisella down at a sewing machine, the extra pedal practically comes into being on its own, because without

it she could not reach the Singer treadle. I know full well
that if I had not added that extra pedal, most of my readers would not have noticed its absence when they read
the description of Gisella using the machine. Moreover, I
myself, were I to read the excerpt after some time had
passed, would not think anything was missing.

Yet something *would* have been missing. A small
space, the size of one foot pedal, would have been exposed in the story. And poor Gisella's foot would be
hanging forever above the Singer treadle, never able to
spin the wheel. It is entirely possible that similar tiny
spaces would have emerged in other parts of the book
too, and in their quiet, hidden way they would have
joined forces to create a bothersome void in the reader's
mind, and a dim suspicion of some negligence on the
part of the author, and even of a breach of trust. But if
the writer allows himself to be Gisella, in body and soul,
if he accepts the rare and wonderful invitation to be such
a Gisella, then the extra pedal will naturally occur, as will
thousands of other sensations and nuances and accessories that the writer gives the characters.

The materialization of these elements is a process
mostly unnoticed by the writer, occurring as naturally as
a tree bearing fruit. When it exists, the writer can give
Gisella—almost without thinking about it—the extra
pedal, and then her foot can reach the machine and she
can make it move, and the pedal can move the large
wheel on the side, and the wheel can spin, and the
wheels of the story can spin too, and the whole fragile

and slightly groundless world, born from a marriage of imagination and reality and words, can begin to move fully and confidently.

When I write a character, I want to know and feel and experience as many characteristics and psychic arrays as possible, including things that are difficult even to name. For example, the character's muscle tone, both physical and emotional: the measure of vitality and alertness and tautness of his or her physical and emotional being. The speed of her thought, the rhythm of his speech, the duration of pauses between her words when she speaks. The roughness of his skin, the touch of her hair. His favorite position, in sex and in sleep.

Not all of these things will end up in the book, of course. I believe it is best for only the tip of the iceberg, only one-tenth of everything the writer knows about his characters, to appear in the book. But the writer must know and feel the other nine-tenths too, even if they remain underwater. Because without them, what surfaces above the water will not have the validity of truth. When these complementary elements exist in the writer's consciousness, they radiate themselves to the visible aspects and serve as a sounding board and a stable foundation for the character, and it is they that give the character its full existence.

I can attest that when I reach that knowledge of the Other from within him—and this does not always occur, not with every character; I wish I could reach it with every character, but regrettably that does not happen—

when I reach that place in the story, I experience one of
the greatest pleasures of writing: the ability to allow my
characters to be themselves—inside me. The writer then
becomes the space within which his characters can fulfill
their characteristics and desires, their urges and acts of
foolishness, madness, and kindness, which the writer
himself is incapable of—because he is a specific, finite
person, and because these characteristics, these desires
and acts, threaten him or somehow contradict him, even
invalidate him.

What marvelous happiness, what sweet reward there
is in these moments, when in the very act of writing a
character, the writer is also written by him or her. Some
unknown option of his personality, an option that was
mute, latent, suppressed, is suddenly articulated to him,
redeemed by a particular character, *brought to light*.

From experience I know how wonderful it is when a
character I have written surprises me this way, or even
betrays me, by acting in contrast to my consciousness
and personality and fears, acting beyond my horizons.
The feeling at those times is one of extraordinary physical and emotional pleasure. In the simplest way, I can say
that it is as though someone grabs me by the back of my
neck with immense vigor and lifts me up, forcing me to
take off outside my own skin.

On a closely related issue, I would like to say a few words
about the meaning of literary writing—as I see it, as I be-

lieve in it—for people who have been living for over a
century in an area that can be described, without exaggeration, as a disaster zone.

First, a clarification: I am not planning to talk "politics," but rather to address the intimate, internal
processes that occur among those who live in a disaster
zone, and the role of literature and writing in a climate as
lethal as the one we live in.

To live in a disaster zone means to be clenched, both
physically and emotionally. The muscles of the body and
the soul are alert and tensed, ready for fight or flight.
Anyone who lives in this condition knows that not only
the body clenches but also the soul, preparing itself
for the next explosion or news bulletin. "He who laughs
has not yet heard the terrible tidings," wrote Bertolt
Brecht—another experienced citizen of disaster zones—
in his poem "To Posterity." Indeed, when one lives in a
disaster zone, one is constantly on guard, and one's entire
being anticipates imminent pain, imminent humiliation.

It is difficult to determine the moment at which the
cruel reversal occurs. When is the question of whether
the pain and humiliation will in fact occur no longer significant because, either way, you are already deep inside
them, even if they themselves remain only possibilities?
For you have already *created* them inside you. You are
already maintaining a routine that is saturated with humiliation because of the constant fear of humiliation. You
no longer realize to what extent your life is largely conducted within the fear of fear, and how much the anxiety

is slowly distorting your nature—as an individual and as a society—and how it is robbing you of your happiness, of your purpose in life.

In this intolerable climate, I and many other writers try to write.

In the first two years of the last intifada, for example, I went into my study every morning and wrote a story about a man and a woman who spend an entire night in a car, on an intense and turbulent journey. There were moments when it seemed utterly mad to shut myself up with these people in the car while the world around me turned upside down. On the other hand, writing has always been the best way for me to stay sane, and to find a grasping point in the world, which, as I grow older, seems more and more illusory and absurd, not truly graspable.

When the book I was writing—*Her Body Knows*—was eventually published, I was frequently asked, "Why didn't you write about the intifada?" "How could it be that the man and the woman are not a Palestinian who falls in love with an Israeli?" And also, "Is the man's broken leg a metaphor for the fracture occurring in the Zionist idea?" And of course, "Is the car really an allegory for the stifling Occupation?"

My reply was, No, these are a man and a woman who insist on turning inward, to each other—because they must. They even turn their backs on the "situation" outside, perhaps because they instinctively feel that this "situation" may cause them to miss out on the most important things in their lives. They feel that because of the "situation" and its terrors, they barely have the time or energy left over to inquire into the greater questions of human existence, and their own private little existence, which happens to have been tossed into the disaster zone of the Middle East.

When we live in a perpetual battle for our very existence, we often begin, out of despair and anxiety, and perhaps mainly out of exhaustion, to believe deep in our hearts that the war—in all its forms and guises—is the main thing in life, and often the only thing. We are so submerged in our warped perception that we barely grasp the true price we are paying for living alongside our own lives, for not daring even to dream about the whole spectrum of possibilities that a full, normal, peaceful life can offer a human being.

Again, I hope you understand that I am not talking "politics" in the narrow and restricted meaning of the term, in its insulting meaning, I would say. I will not discuss occupied territories or settlements or unilateral or bilateral withdrawals today. But I will talk of the principles of this disastrous condition, and of the roots it is striking in us, and the blows it is delivering us. Moreover, I will address the role of literature in this state, the healing and mending that literary writing and a literary way of thinking, observing, and regarding can bring to these distortions.

In the almost-eternal disaster zone in which our lives are lived, if we dare for a moment to truly look at what is happening to us and to those around us, we will be forced to admit that, essentially, we are always preparing ourselves for the next disaster. In this perpetual state of preparation, we unconsciously reduce within ourselves, one by one, our human elements and qualities, so that when they are taken from us, or debased by the situation or by the enemy, we will suffer less. Because if my gut feeling, and yours, is right, if it is true that in this terrible situation "he who feels more, suffers more," then this aphorism is gradually translated in our minds into "he who feels, suffers." We are so afraid of death that we condense the range of our emotional, psychic vitality.

In a disaster zone, of course, or in a prolonged war, the tendency of the hawkish sides is to minimize and deny the human aspect of the enemy, to flatten it into a stereotype or a collection of prejudices. Because only then can one truly fight to the death for decades, eventually hoping for the enemy's disappearance or death, believing that he is less human than us, or completely nonhuman.

And please, do not tell me that life here is more or less normal or tolerable, that we have grown accustomed to the periodic, cyclical wars, and that we have learned to make the best of our existence in this cruel region. One cannot truly adapt to such warped conditions without paying a high price, the highest price of all—the price of living itself, the price of sensitivity, of humanity, of curiosity, and of liberty of thought. The fear of and aversion to facing others fully and soberly: not only the enemy, but *any others*.

After spending a century in all-out war and becoming

accustomed to seeing anyone who threatens us as an enemy to the death, and having the concept of "enemy" ingrained in us so deeply, almost from birth, and living in
an environment in which the concept is so highly avail-
able, because of the hostility and the constant acts of violence—after all this, eventually our compasses and
healthy instincts go awry, and then, in almost any situation of conflict and disagreement, even one's brother
looks like the enemy. It is enough for his opinions and
habits to be different from our own, for his desires to be
distinct from our own, for his interpretation of a situation
to be different from ours, for our brother to become, in
our minds, in our fears, an enemy.

When I say this, I fear that after decades of spending
most of our energies, our thoughts and attention and in-
ventiveness, our blood and our life and our financial
means, on protecting our external borders, fortifying and
safeguarding them more and more—after all this, we may
be very close to becoming like a suit of armor that no
longer contains a knight, no longer contains a *human*.
Moreover, I often think that even if this longed-for peace
reaches our region tomorrow, in some sense it will
already be too late. Because the qualities and the viewpoints and the behaviors that the violence has formulated in us, Israelis and Palestinians, will continue to
work their ways on us for many more years. They will
not be quick to disintegrate in our bloodstream, both private and national, and they will keep on poisoning our
souls, sabotaging the possibility of maintaining a stable

peace. Time after time, they will sweep us away and cause us to replay all the same old ills, which will, in turn, create more and more waves of violence.

Let us return to literature for one more moment.

The purpose of literature is the complete opposite of what I have described thus far: in literary writing, we do everything we can to redeem each character in our story from alienation and impersonality, from the grip of stereotypes and prejudices. When we write a story, we struggle—for years, sometimes—to comprehend all the facets of one human character: its internal contradictions, its motives and inhibitions, the boiling magma I talked of earlier.

There is something tender, almost maternal, in the way a writer attunes all his senses, his consciousness and subconscious, his dreams and waking states, to every emotional current and sensation that passes through the characters he has created. There is something naked and exposed, a self-abandonment, in the writer's willingness to give himself over, unprotected, to the inner workings of the character he is writing about—and, I almost said, communing with.

To write a novel is, to a great extent, to be totally responsible for a few dozen characters. No one will volunteer to write them for us. No one will breathe life into them for us. Sometimes I liken this to a person who is hiding a huge family, several dozen strong, in the cellar beneath his house during a war. This person must go down to the cellar at least once a day to bring food and water to the people. Once in a while he must talk with them about their conditions, try to alleviate their stress, settle the quarrels that erupt among them, offer practical solutions for their immediate troubles. It would also be good of him to tell them about what is going on in the world, listen to their stories and recollections, remind them of all the things they can dream about, and the things they miss, so that they can briefly forget the stifling pit they are trapped in. And then, after doing all these kind things, he must remove their chamber pots and empty them out. Only this person can do all these things; no one can do them for him.

This is exactly the role an author plays for his characters: with all his might, with all his talent and empathy, he must exist in their space—the entire range of human activity that occurs between spiritual talk and the emptying of chamber pots. He must be completely attentive to all their needs, both the spiritual and the corporeal. He must devote himself to them. Body and soul.

If there is one thing I would hope that politics, and politicians and statesmen, might learn from literature, it is this mode of dedication to the situation and to the people trapped in it—after all, they bear significant responsibility for creating the traps, and for the conditions of those trapped. If they are not capable of true dedication, we can demand at the very least that they provide this form of attentiveness, of purposefulness, which is invaluable for reviving the person inside the suit of armor.

By doing so, we remind ourselves again and again of a
banal fact that turns out to be so easily forgotten and denied: that behind the armor is a human being. Behind
our armor, and behind our enemy's. Behind the armor of
fear, indifference, hatred, and the constriction of the
soul; behind everything that languishes within each one
of us as these difficult years go by; behind all the fortified
walls—there is *a human being*.

The violence in which we have been living for so long
acts naturally and incessantly to turn human beings into
faceless, one dimensional creatures lacking volition.
Wars, armies, regimes, and fanatic religions try to blur
the nuances that create personal, private uniqueness, the
nonrecurrent wonder of each and every person, and attempt to turn people into a mass, into a horde, so that
they may be better "suited" to their purposes and to the
entire situation. Literature—and not necessarily any particular book, but the attentiveness engendered by direct,
profound, complex literature—reminds us of our duty to
demand for ourselves—from the "situation"—the right
to individuality and uniqueness. It helps us to reclaim
some of the things that this "situation" tries relentlessly
to expropriate: the subtle, discerning application to the
person trapped in the conflict, whether friend or foe; the
complex nuances of relationships between people and
between different communities; the precision of words
and descriptions; the flexibility of thought; the ability and
the courage to occasionally change the point of view in
which we are frozen (sometimes fossilized); the deep and
essential understanding that we can—we must—read

every human situation from several different points of view.

Then we may be able to reach the place in which the totally contradictory stories of different people, different nations, even sworn enemies, may coexist and play out together. This is the place where we are finally able to grasp that in true negotiations, our wishes will be forced to encounter the Other's, forced to recognize their just-ness, their legitimacy. This is the moment when we feel the sharp growing pains that always attend the arrival of sobriety, and in this case the realization that there is a limit to our ability to mold reality so that it perfectly suits only our own needs. This is the moment when we feel what I called earlier "the principle of Otherness," whose deep-seated meaning, if you wish, is the rightful exis-tence, the stories, pains, and hopes, of the Other. If we can only reach this Archimedean point, we can begin to dismantle the barriers and detonators that prevent us from solving the conflict.

Because when we know the Other from within him—even if that Other is our enemy—we can never again be completely indifferent to him. Something inside us be-comes committed to him, or at least to his complexities. It becomes difficult for us to completely deny him or cancel him out as "not human." We can no longer em-ploy our usual ease and expertise to avoid his suffering, his justice, his *story*. Perhaps we can even be a little more tolerant of his mistakes. For we then see these mis-takes as part of his tragedy. And if we have any strength

and generosity remaining, we can even create a situation
in which it is easier for our enemy to step out of his own
traps; we too may benefit from this.

To write about the enemy means, primarily, to think
about the enemy, and this is a requirement for anyone
who has an enemy, even if he is absolutely convinced of
his own justness and the enemy's malice and cruelty. To
think (or to write) about the enemy does not necessarily
mean to justify him. I cannot, for example, contemplate
writing about a Nazi character in such a way as to justify him, although I felt an urge—even an obligation—to
write, in *See Under: Love*, about a Nazi officer, so that I
could understand how a normal person becomes a Nazi,
how he justifies his acts to himself, and what processes
he goes through in doing so.

Sartre's exploration of why we write, in his essay
What Is Literature? is relevant here: "Nobody can suppose for a moment that it is possible to write a good
novel in praise of anti-Semitism. For, the moment I feel
that my freedom is indissolubly linked with that of all
other men, it cannot be demanded of me that I use it to
approve the enslavement of a part of these men. Thus,
whether he is an essayist, a pamphleteer, a satirist, or
a novelist, whether he speaks only of individual pas-
sions or whether he attacks the social order, the writer, a
free man addressing free men, has only one subject—
freedom."

Sartre may have been naive in his assertion that "nobody can suppose for a moment that it is possible to write a good novel in praise of anti-Semitism"; such books have been written and will probably continue to be written. But he was certainly right about the topic that preoccupies authors, and which is also the soul of literature—freedom. The freedom to think differently, to see things differently. And this includes seeing the enemy differently.

To think about the enemy, then. To think about him gravely and with deep attentiveness. Not merely to hate or fear him, but to think of him as a person or a society or a nation that is separate from us and from our own fears and hopes, from our beliefs and modes of thought and interests and wounds. To allow the enemy to be an Other, with all this entails. Such an outlook may also be militarily advantageous from an intelligence point of view: "Know thy enemy—from within him." It could also help us alter reality itself, so that the enemy gradually ceases to be our enemy.

I would like to clarify that I am not referring to the maxim "Love thy enemy." I cannot claim to have been blessed with such noble magnanimity (and I always find it somewhat suspect when I encounter it in others). But I am certainly speaking of a sincere effort to try to *understand* the enemy, his motives, his internal logic, his worldview, and the story he tells himself.

Of course, it is not easy to read reality through the enemy's eyes. It is difficult and frightening to give up our sophisticated defense mechanisms and be exposed to the feelings with which the enemy experiences the conflict and how, in fact, he experiences us. Taking such a step challenges our faith in ourselves and in our own justness. It poses a danger of undermining "the official story"—usually the only permissible, "legitimate" story—that a frightened nation, a nation at war, always tells itself. But perhaps we can upend the previous sentence and say that sometimes a nation remains in a prolonged state of struggle precisely because it is trapped, for generations sometimes, within a particular "official story"?

————

There is one other clear advantage to observing reality through the enemy's eyes. The enemy sees in us, in the nation facing him, the things that each of us always shows an enemy: cruelty, aggression, brutality, self-righteousness, self-pity. We are often unaware of everything we "project" onto the enemy, and thereby onto others as well, even those who are not our enemy—and eventually onto ourselves too.

Not infrequently, we tell ourselves that we are taking a certain course of action, committing an act of violence or brutality, only because we are in a state of war, and that when the war is over we will go right back to being the moral, upstanding society we used to be. But we must consider the possibility that the enemy—toward whom we direct these hostile and violent acts, and who thereby becomes their permanent victim—senses long before we do how much these behaviors have become an integral part of our being as a nation and as a society, and

how deeply they have seeped into our innermost systems. It is also possible that reversing our point of view,
by looking at ourselves through the eyes of the nation we
are occupying, for example, can sound the alarm bells
within us, enabling us to understand, before it is too late,
the depth of our denial, our destructiveness, and our
blindness. We will know then what we have to save ourselves from, and how essential it is *for ourselves* to
change the situation profoundly.

When we are able to read the text of reality through
our enemy's eyes, it becomes more complex, more realistic, allowing us to recover the elements we suspended
from our world picture. From that moment, reality is
more than just a projection of our fears and desires and
illusions: when we are capable of seeing the story of the
Other through his eyes, we are in healthier and more
valid contact with the facts. We then have a far greater
chance to avoid making critical mistakes and perceiving
events in a self-centered, clenched, and restricted way.
And then, sometimes, we can also grasp—in a way we
never previously allowed ourselves to—that this mythological, menacing, and demonic enemy is no more than
an amalgamation of people who are as frightened, tormented, and despondent as we are. This comprehension,
to me, is the essential beginning of any process of sobriety and reconciliation.

———

These are some of the counsels that literature can offer
to politics and to those engaged in politics, and in fact to

anyone coping with an arbitrary and violent reality. The advice may sound weak and out of touch today, against the clamor of war that surrounds us, but the principles are valid for novel-writing, for interpersonal relationships, and for delineating policies—of peace or of war.

This approach to ourselves, to the enemy, to the entire conflict, and to our lives within it, an approach I have broadly termed "the literary approach," is to me, more than anything, an act of redefining ourselves as human beings in a situation whose essence and methodology consist entirely of dehumanization. It can once again remind us of everything we hold dear that is now in danger, and it can restore something of the humanity that was swiftly and violently robbed from us, in a process whose severity we were not always aware of. Insisting on such an approach can also, slowly but surely, put us on the road to sincere dialogue with our enemies, a dialogue that will lead, one hopes, to reconciliation and peace.

January 2006

Writing in the Dark

"Our personal happiness or unhappiness, our 'terrestrial' condition, is of great importance for the things we write," says Natalia Ginzburg in *It's Hard to Talk About Yourself*, in a chapter in which she discusses her life and writing after a deep personal tragedy.

It is hard to talk about yourself, and so before I reflect on my writing experience now, at this time in my life, let me say a few words about the effects of a trauma, a disaster situation, on a society and on a nation as a whole.

The words of the mouse from Kafka's short story "A Little Fable" come to mind. As the trap closes in on the mouse and the cat prowls beyond, he says, "Alas, the world is growing smaller every day." After many years of living in an extreme and violent state of political, military, and religious conflict, I am sad to report that Kafka's mouse was right: the world is indeed growing smaller, growing narrower, every day. I can also tell you about the void that slowly emerges between the individual and the violent, chaotic state that encompasses practically every aspect of his life.

This void does not remain empty. It quickly fills up with apathy, cynicism, and above all despair—the despair that can fuel a distorted reality for many years, sometimes generations. The despair that one will never manage to change the situation, never redeem it. And the deepest despair of all—the despair of human beings, of what the distorted situation ultimately exposes in each of us.

I feel the heavy price that I and the people around me pay for this prolonged state of war. Part of this price is a shrinking of our soul's surface area—those parts of us that touch the violent, menacing world outside—and a diminished ability and willingness to empathize at all with other people in pain. We also pay the price by suspending our moral judgment, and we give up on understanding what we ourselves think. Given a situation so frightening, so deceptive, and so complicated—both morally and practically—we feel it may be better not to think or know. Better to hand over the job of thinking and doing and setting moral standards to those who are surely "in the know." Better not to feel too much until the crisis ends—and if it never ends, at least we'll have suffered a little less, developed a useful dullness, protected ourselves as much as we could with a little indifference, a little repression, a little deliberate blindness, and a large dose of self-anesthetics.

The constant—and very real—fear of being hurt, the fear of death, of intolerable loss, or even of "mere" humiliation, leads each of us, the citizens and prisoners of the conflict, to dampen our own vitality, our emotional and intellectual range, and to cloak ourselves in more and more protective layers until we suffocate.

Kafka's mouse was right: when your predator closes in on you, your world does get smaller. So does the language that describes it.

From experience I can say that the language used by the citizens of a conflict to describe their situation becomes flatter and flatter as the conflict goes on, gradually evolving into a series of clichés and slogans. It starts with the jargon invented by the systems that handle the conflict directly—the army, the police, the bureaucracy. The trend spreads into the mass media, which create an elaborate, shrewd language designed to tell their audiences the most palatable story (thereby erecting a barrier between everything the state does in the twilight zone of the conflict and the way its citizens choose to see themselves). The process eventually seeps into the private, intimate language of the citizens (even if they vehemently deny it).

The evolution is all too understandable: human language's natural richness and its ability to touch on the finest nuances of existence can be truly hurtful in a state of conflict because they constantly remind us of the exuberant reality that we have lost, of its complexities and subtleties. The more hopeless the situation seems and the shallower the language becomes, the more public discourse dwindles, until all that remains are tired recriminations between the enemies or between political adversaries within the state. All that remains are the clichés we use to describe the enemy and ourselves—the prejudices, mythological anxieties, and crude generalizations with which we trap ourselves and ensnare our enemies. The world indeed grows smaller.

These thoughts are relevant not only to the conflict in the Middle East. In so many parts of the world today billions of people face some threat to the existence, the values, the liberty, and the identity of human beings. Almost every one of us faces his own threat, his own curse. Each of us feels—or can guess—how his unique "situation" may quickly become a trap that will rob his freedom, his sense of home in his country, his private language, his free will.

In this reality, we authors and poets write. In Israel and in Palestine, in Chechnya and in Sudan, in New York and in the Congo. There are times in my workday, after a few hours of writing, when I look up and think: Now, at this very moment, sits another author, whom I do not know, in Damascus or Tehran, in Kigali or Dublin, who, like me, is engaged in the strange, baseless, wonderful work of creation, within a reality that contains so much violence and alienation, indifference and diminishment. I have a distant ally who does not know me, and together we are weaving this shapeless web, which nonetheless has immense power, the power to change a world and create a world, the power to give words to the mute and to bring about *tikkun*—"repair"—in the deepest, kabbalistic sense of the word.

———

As for myself, in the works of fiction I have written in recent years, I have almost intentionally turned my back on the immediate, burning reality of my country, the reality of the latest news bulletin. I have written books about this reality in the past, and I have never stopped discussing it and trying to understand it through essays, articles, and interviews. I have taken part in dozens of protests and international peace initiatives. I have met with my neighbors—some of whom were my enemies—every time I thought there was any chance for dialogue. Yet over the past few years, out of a decision that is almost a protest, I have not written about these disaster zones in my *literature*.

Why? Because I wanted to write about other things, things no less important, things for which it's hard to find the time, the emotion, and the total attention, while the near-eternal war thunders on outside. I wrote about a husband's obsessive jealousy of his wife, about homeless children on the streets of Jerusalem, about a man and a woman who establish a private, almost hermetic language within their reverie of love. I wrote about the loneliness of Samson, the biblical hero, I wrote about the subtle and tangled relationships between women and their mothers, and between children and parents in general.

Roughly four years ago, when my second son was

about to enlist in the army, I could no longer remain where I was. I was overcome with an almost physical sense of urgency and alarm that gave me no rest. I began then to write a novel that deals directly with the difficult reality I live in, a novel that describes how the cruelty of the external situation invades the delicate, intimate fabric of one family, ultimately tearing it to shreds.

"At the moment someone is writing," says Natalia Ginzburg, "he is miraculously driven to forget the immediate circumstances of his own life . . . But whether we are happy or unhappy leads us to write in one way or another. When we are happy our imagination is stronger; when we are unhappy our memory works with greater vitality."

It is hard to talk about yourself. I will only say what I can say at this time, from where I stand now.

I write. The consciousness of the disaster that befell me upon the death of my son Uri in the Second Lebanon War now permeates every minute of my life. The power of memory is indeed great and heavy, and at times has a paralyzing effect. Nevertheless, the act of writing creates for me a "space" of sorts, an emotional expanse that I have never known before, where death is more than the absolute, unambiguous opposite of life.

The authors who are here today know: when we write, we feel the world in flux, elastic, full of possibilities—unfrozen. Anywhere the human element exists, there is no freezing and no paralysis, and there is no status quo (even if we sometimes mistakenly think there

is; even if there are those who would very much like us to
think there is).

I write, and the world does not close in on me. It
does not grow smaller. It moves in the direction of what
is open, future, possible.

I imagine, and the act of imagination revives me. I
am not fossilized or paralyzed in the face of predators. I
invent characters. Sometimes I feel as if I am digging
people out of the ice in which reality has encased them.
But perhaps, more than anything, the person I am digging out at the moment is myself.

I write. I feel the many possibilities that exist in every
human situation, and I feel my capacity to choose among
them. I feel the sweetness of liberty, which I thought I
had lost. I take pleasure in the richness of a real, personal, intimate language. I remember the delights of
breathing fully, properly, when I manage to escape the
claustrophobia of slogans and clichés. I begin to breathe
with both lungs.

I write, and I feel that the correct and accurate use of
words acts like a medicine. It purifies the air I breathe,
removes the pollutants, and frustrates the schemes of
language defrauders and language rapists. I write and
feel my sensitivity to language and my intimacy with its
different layers, with its sensuality and humor, restore
me to myself, to the person I was before my selfhood was
expropriated by the conflict, by the governments and the
armies, by the despair and the tragedy.

I write. I purge myself of one of the dubious but typ-

ical talents that arise in a state of war—the talent for being an enemy, nothing but an enemy. I write, and I try
not to shield myself from the legitimacy and the suffering of my enemy, or from the tragedy and the complexity
of his life, or from his mistakes and crimes, or from
knowing what I myself am doing to him. Nor do I shelter
myself from the surprising similarities I discover between him and me.

I write. And all at once I am no longer doomed to
face this absolute, false, suffocating dichotomy—this in-
human choice between "victim" and "aggressor," without
any third, more human option. When I write, I can be a
whole person, with natural passages between my various
parts, and with some parts that feel close to the suffering
and the just assertions of my enemies without giving up
my own identity at all.

At times, in the course of writing, I can remember
what we all felt in Israel for one rare moment, when
Egyptian president Anwar Sadat's plane landed in Tel
Aviv after decades of war between the two nations. We
suddenly discovered how heavy the burden was that we
had been carrying all our lives—the burden of hostility
and fear and suspicion. The burden of having to always
be on guard, to always be an enemy, all the time. How
blissful it was in that moment to do away with the massive armor of suspicion, hatred, and prejudice. How
frighteningly blissful it was to stand naked, to stand pure,
and watch as before our eyes a human face emerged
from the narrow, one-dimensional depiction we had
been seeing for years.

I write, and I give my most private and intimate names to an external, unknown world. In some sense, I make it mine. So do I return from a land of exile and alienation—I come home. I change, just slightly, what previously seemed unchangeable. Even when I describe the cruelest arbitrariness that determines my fate— whether man-made or preordained—I suddenly find in it new subtleties and nuances. I find that simply writing about the arbitrariness lets me move freely in its presence. That the very fact of standing up against the arbitrariness gives me freedom—perhaps the only freedom man has against any kind of arbitrariness—the freedom to articulate the tragedy of my situation *in my own words*. The freedom to articulate myself differently, freshly, against the unbending dictates of arbitrariness that threaten to bind me and pin me down.

I also write about what cannot be restored. About what has no comfort. Then too, in a way I still cannot explain, the circumstances of my life do not close in on me and leave me paralyzed. Many times a day, as I sit at my writing desk, I touch sorrow and loss like someone touching electricity with bare hands, yet it does not kill me. I do not understand how this miracle has come to pass. Perhaps after I finish this novel, I will try to understand. Not now. It is too soon.

I write the life of my country, Israel. A tortured country, drugged to the point of overdose by history, by emotions beyond what humans can contain, by an extreme excess of events and tragedy, by an excess of fear and a crippling sobriety, by an excess of memory, by dashed hopes, by a fate unique among nations. It is an existence that sometimes seems to take on the proportions of a mythic tale, diminishing our prospects of ever living an ordinary life as a state.

We authors know periods of despair and self-loathing. Our work, fundamentally, entails dismantling personalities and relinquishing some of our most effective defense mechanisms. Willingly we struggle with the hardest, ugliest, rawest, and most painful matters of the soul. Our work forces us, again and again, to acknowledge our helplessness as people and as artists.

Yet still—and this is the great miracle, the alchemy of our act—in some sense, from the moment we take pen in hand or put fingers to keyboard, we have already ceased to be a victim at the mercy of all that enslaved and restricted us before we began writing.

We write. How fortunate we are: The world does not close in on us. The world does not grow smaller.

The Arthur Miller Freedom to Write Lecture, New York, April 24, 2007

Individual Language and Mass Language

To open the International Literature Festival Berlin as an Israeli author is not only a great honor, but also a conjuncture that would have been unthinkable until not so many years ago, and even today I cannot be indifferent to its significance.

Despite the close relationship between Israel and Germany today—and between Israelis and Germans, between Jews and Germans—even now there is a place in one's mind and in one's heart where certain statements must be filtered through the prisms of time and memory to be refracted into the entire spectrum of colors and shades. As I stand here before you in Berlin, I cannot help but begin with the thoughts that are constantly refracted within me, in that prism of time and memory.

I was born and raised in Jerusalem, in a neighborhood and in a family in which people could not even utter the word "Germany." They found it difficult to say "Holocaust" too, and spoke only of "what happened *over there.*"

It is interesting to note that in Hebrew, Yiddish, and every other language they speak, when Jewish people refer to the Holocaust, they tend to talk about "what happened *over there*," whereas non-Jews usually speak in terms of "what happened *then*." There is a vast difference between "there" and "then." "Then" means in the past tense; "then" enfolds within it something that happened and ended, and is no longer. While "there," conversely, suggests that somewhere out there, in the distance, the thing that happened is still occurring, constantly growing stronger alongside our daily lives, and that it may re-erupt. It is not decisively over. Certainly not for us, the Jews.

As a child, I often heard the term "the Nazi beast," and when I asked the adults who this beast was, they refused to tell me, and said there were things a child should not know. Years later, I wrote in *See Under: Love* about Momik, the son of Holocaust survivors who never tell him what really happened to them "Over There." The frightened Momik imagines the Nazi beast as a monster that controlled a land called "Over There," where it tortured the people Momik loves and did things to them that hurt them forever and denied them the ability to live a full life.

When I was four or five, I heard for the first time of Simon Wiesenthal, the Nazi-hunter. I felt a great sense of relief: Finally, I thought, there is someone courageous enough to fight the beast, even willing to hunt it down! Had I known how to write at the time, I might have written Wiesenthal a letter full of the detailed and practical questions that were preoccupying me, because I imagined that this hunter probably knew everything about his prey.

My generation, the children of the early 1950s in Israel, lived in a thick and densely populated silence. In my neighborhood, people screamed every night from their nightmares. More than once, when we walked into a room where adults were telling stories of the war, the conversation stopped immediately. We did pick up the occasional fragment: "The last time I saw him was on Himmelstrasse in Treblinka," or, "She lost both her children in the first *Aktion*."

Every day, at twenty minutes past one, there was a ten-minute program on the radio in which a female announcer with a glum and rhythmic voice read the names of people searching for relatives lost during the war and in the Holocaust: *Rachel, daughter of Perla and Abraham Seligson from Przemyśl, is looking for her little sister Leah'leh, who lived in Warsaw between the years . . . Eliyahu Frumkin, son of Yocheved and Hershl Frumkin from Stry, is looking for his wife, Elisheva, née Eichel, and his two sons, Yaakov and Meir . . .* And so on and so forth. Every lunch of my childhood was spent listening to the sounds of this quiet lament.

When I was seven, the Eichmann trial was held in Jerusalem, and then we listened to the radio during dinner when they broadcast descriptions of the horrors. You could say that my generation lost its appetite, but

there was another loss too. It was the loss of something
deeper, which we did not understand at the time, of
course, and which is still being deciphered throughout
the course of our lives. Perhaps what we lost was the illusion of our parents' power to protect us from the terrors
of life. Or perhaps we lost our faith in the possibility that
we, the Jews, would ever live a complete, secure life, like
all other nations. And perhaps, above all, we felt the loss
of the natural, childlike faith—faith in man, in his kindness, in his compassion.

About two decades ago, when my oldest son was
three, his preschool commemorated Holocaust Memorial Day, as it did every year. My son did not understand
much of what he was told, and he came home confused
and frightened. "Dad, what are Nazis? What did they
do? Why did they do it?" And I did not want to tell him.
I, who had grown up within the silence and fragmented
whispers that had filled me with so many fears and nightmares, who had written a book about a boy who almost
loses his mind because of his parents' silence, suddenly
understood my parents and my friends' parents who
chose to be mute.

I felt that if I told him, if I even so much as cautiously
alluded to what had happened *over there*, something in
the purity of my three-year-old son would be polluted;
that from the moment such possibilities of cruelty were
formulated in his childlike, innocent consciousness, he
would never again be the same child.

He would no longer be a child at all.

When I published *See Under: Love* in Israel, some critics wrote that I belonged to the "second generation" and that I was the son of "Holocaust survivors." I am not. My father immigrated to Palestine from Poland as a child, in 1936. My mother was born in Palestine, before the State of Israel was established.

And yet I am. I am the son of "Holocaust survivors" because in my home too, as in so many Israeli homes, a thread of deep anxiety was stretched out, and with almost every move you made, you touched it. Even if you were very careful, even if you hardly made any unnecessary movements, you still felt that constant quiver of a profound lack of confidence in the possibility of existence. A suspicion toward man and what might erupt from him at any moment.

In our home too, at every celebration, with every purchase of a new piece of furniture, every time a new child was born in the neighborhood, there was a feeling that each such event was one more word, one more sentence, in the intensely conducted dialogue with *over there*. That every presence echoed an absence, and that life, the simplest of daily routines, the most trivial oscillations— "Should the child be allowed to go on the school trip?" or "Is it worth renovating the apartment?"—somehow echoed what happened *over there*: all those things that managed to survive the *there*, and all those that did not; and the life lessons, the acute knowledge that had been burned in our memory.

This became all the more pertinent when greater

decisions were at stake: Which profession should we choose? Should we vote right-wing or left-wing? Marry or stay single? Have another child, or is one enough? Should we even bring a child into this world? All these decisions and acts, small and large, amounted to a huge, practically superhuman effort to weave the thin fabric of everydayness over the horrors beneath. An effort to convince ourselves that despite everything we know, despite everything engraved on our bodies and souls, we have the capacity to live on, and to keep choosing life and human existence.

Because for people like myself, born in Israel in the years after the Holocaust, the primary feeling—about which we could not talk at all, and for which we may not have had the words at the time—was that for us, for Jews, death was the immediate interlocutor. That life, even when it was full of the energies and hopes and fruitfulness of a newly revived young country, still involved an enormous and constant effort to escape the dread of death.

You may say, with good reason, that this is in fact the basic human condition. Certainly it is so, but for us it had daily and pressing reminders, open wounds and fresh scars, and representatives who were living and tangible, their bodies and souls crushed.

In Israel of the 1950s and '60s, and not only during times of extreme despair but precisely at those moments when the great commotion of "nation-building" waned, in the moments when we tired a little, just for an instant, of being a miracle of renewal and re-creation, in those moments of the twilight of the soul, both private and national, we could immediately feel, in the most intimate way, the band of frost that suddenly tightens around our hearts and says quietly but firmly: How quickly life fades. How fragile it all is. The body, the family. Death is true, all else is an illusion.

Ever since knowing I would be an author, I knew I would write about the Holocaust. I think these two convictions came to me at the same time. Perhaps also because from a very young age I had the feeling that all the many books I had read about the Holocaust had left unanswered a few simple but essential questions. I had to ask these questions of myself, and I had to reply in my own words.

As I grew up, I became increasingly aware that I could not truly understand my life in Israel, as a man, as a father, as a writer, as an Israeli, as a Jew, until I wrote about my unlived life, *over there*, in the Holocaust. And about what would have happened to me had I been *over there* as a victim, and as one of the murderers.

I wanted to know *both* these things. One was not enough.

Namely: If I had been a Jew under the Nazi regime, a Jew in a concentration camp or a death camp, what could I have done to save something of myself, of my selfhood, in a reality in which people were stripped not only of their clothes but also of their names, so that they became—to others—numbers tattooed on an arm? A re-

ality in which people's previous lives were taken away
from them—their family, their friends, their profession,
their loves, their talents. A reality in which millions of
people were relegated, by other human beings, to the
lowest rung of existence: to being nothing more than
flesh and blood intended for destruction with the utmost
efficiency.

What was the thing inside me that I could hold up
against this attempt at erasure? What was the thing that
could preserve the human spark within me, in a reality
entirely aimed at extinguishing it?

One can answer this question only about one's self, in
private. But perhaps I can suggest a possible path to the
answer. In the Jewish tradition there is a legend, or a belief, that every person has a small bone in his body called
the *luz*, located at the tip of the spine, which enfolds the
essence of a person's soul. This bone cannot be de-
stroyed. Even if the entire human body is shattered,
crushed, or burned, the *luz* bone does not perish. It
stores a person's spark of uniqueness, the core of his selfhood. According to the belief, this bone will be the
source of man's resurrection.

Those of you who would like to find your own response to the question may, when you go home, choose
to gather your thoughts and consider: What is the thing
within me that is the true root of my soul? What is the
quality, the essence, the final spark that will remain in
me even when all other things are extinguished? What is
the thing that has such great and concerted power that I

will be re-created out of it, in an extremely private sort of "big bang"?

Once in a while I ask people close to me what they believe their *luz* is, and I have heard many varied answers. Several writers, and artists in general, have told me that their *luz* is creativity, the passion to create and the urge to produce. Religious people, believers, have often said that their *luz* is the divine spark they feel inside. One friend answered, after much thought: Parenthood, fatherhood. And another friend immediately replied that her *luz* was her longing for the things and people she missed. A woman who was roughly ninety at the time talked about the love of her life, a man who committed suicide over sixty years ago: he was her *luz*.

———

The second question I asked while writing *See Under: Love* is closely related to the first one, and in some ways even derives from it: I asked myself how an ordinary, normal person—as most Nazis and their supporters were—becomes part of a mass-murder apparatus. In other words, what is the thing that I must suspend within myself, that I must dull, repress, so that I can ultimately collaborate with a mechanism of murder? What must I kill within me to be capable of killing another person or people, to desire the destruction of an entire people, or to silently accept it?

Perhaps I should ask this question even more pointedly: Am I myself, consciously or unconsciously, actively

or passively, through indifference or with mute acceptance, collaborating at this very moment with some process that is destined to wreak havoc on another human
being, or on another group of people?

"The death of one man is a tragedy," Stalin said, "but
the death of millions is only statistics." How do tragedies
become statistics for us? I am not saying, of course, that
we are all murderers. Of course not. Yet it seems that
most of us manage to lead a life of almost total indifference to the suffering of entire nations, near and far, and
to the distress of hundreds of millions of human beings
who are poor and hungry and weak and sick, whether in
our own countries or in other parts of the world. We are
capable of developing apathy and alienation toward the
suffering of the foreigners who come to work for us, and
toward the misery of people under occupation—ours,
and others'—and toward the anguish of billions of people living under any kind of dictatorship or enslavement.

With wondrous ease we create the necessary mechanisms to separate ourselves from the suffering of others.
Intellectually and emotionally, we manage to detach the
causal relationship between, for example, our economic
affluence—in the sated and prosperous Western countries—and the poverty of others. Between our own luxu-
ries and the shameful working conditions of others.
Between our air-conditioned, motorized quality of life
and the ecological disasters it brings about.

These "Others" live in such appalling conditions that
they are not usually able to even ask the questions I am

asking here. After all, it is not only genocide that can eradicate a person's *luz*: hunger, poverty, disease, and refugee status can defile and slowly kill the soul of an individual, and sometimes of a whole people.

There are many terrible things occurring not far from us, for which we are unwilling to take any personal responsibility, either through active involvement or through empathy. It is convenient for us, where the burden of personal responsibility is concerned, to become part of a crowd, a faceless crowd with no identity, seemingly free from responsibility and absolved of blame.

Perhaps it is only in this global reality, where so much of our life is lived in a mass dimension, that we can be so indifferent to mass destruction. For it is the very same indifference that the vast majority of the world displays time after time, whether during the Armenian Holocaust or the Jewish Holocaust, in Rwanda or in Bosnia, in the Congo, in Darfur, and in many other places.

And perhaps, then, this is the great question that people living in this age must relentlessly ask themselves: In what state, at which moment, do I become part of the faceless crowd, "the masses"?

There are a number of ways to describe the process whereby the individual is swallowed up in the crowd, or agrees to hand over parts of himself to mass control. Since we, here, are people of literature and language, I will choose the one closest to our interests and to our way of life: I become part of "the masses" when I give up the right to think and formulate my own words, in my

own language, instead accepting automatically and un-
critically the formulations and language that others dic-
tate.

I become "the masses" when I stop formulating my
own choices and the moral compromises I make. When I
stop articulating them over and over again, with fresh
new words each time, words that have not yet eroded in
me, not yet congealed in me, which I cannot ignore or
defend myself against, and which force me to face the
decisions I have made, and to pay the price for them.

The masses, as we know, cannot exist without *mass
language*—a language that will consolidate the multitude
and spur it on to act in a certain way, formulating justifi-
cations for its acts and simplifying the moral and emotional contradictions it may encounter. In other words,
the language of the masses is a language intended to liberate the individual from responsibility for his actions, to
temporarily sever his private, individual judgment from
his sound logic and natural sense of justice.

————

The values and horizons of our world, the atmosphere
that prevails in it and the language that dominates it, are
dictated to a great extent by what is known as mass media, or mass communication. The term "mass media" was
coined in the 1920s, when sociologists began to refer
to "mass society." But are we truly aware of the significance of this term today, and of the process it has gone
through? Do we consider the fact not only that, to a large

extent, the "mass media" today are media designed for the masses, but that in many ways they also *turn their consumers into the masses*?

They do so with the belligerence and the cynicism that emanate from all their manifestations; with their shallow, vulgar language; with the oversimplification and self-righteousness with which they handle complex political and moral problems; with the kitsch in which they douse everything they touch—the kitsch of war and death, the kitsch of love, the kitsch of intimacy.

A cursory look would indicate that these kinds of media actually focus on particular personas rather than on the masses. On the individual rather than on the collective. But this is a dangerous illusion: although mass media emphasize and even sanctify the individual, and seem to direct the individual more and more toward himself, they are ultimately directing him *only* toward himself—his own needs, his clear and narrow interests. In an endless variety of ways, both open and hidden, they liberate him from what he is already eager to shed: responsibility for the consequences of his actions on others. And the moment they anesthetize this responsibility in him, they also dull his political, social, and moral awareness, molding him into conveniently submissive raw material for their own manipulations and those of other interested parties. In other words, they turn him into one of the masses.

These forms of media—written, electronic, online, often free, highly accessible, highly influential—have an existential need to preserve the public's interest, to constantly stimulate its hungry desires. And so even when ostensibly dealing with issues of moral and human import, and even when ostensibly assuming a role of social responsibility, still the finger they point at hotbeds of corruption and wrongdoing and suffering seems mechanical, automatic, with no sincere interest in the problems it highlights. Their true purpose—apart from generating profits for their owners—is to preserve a continually stimulated state of "public condemnation" or "public exoneration" of certain individuals, who change at the speed of light. This rapid exchange is the message of mass media. Sometimes it seems that it is not the information itself that the media deem essential, but merely the rate at which it shifts. The neurotic, covetous, consumerist, seductive beat they create. The zeitgeist: the zapping is the message.

––––––

In this world I have described, literature has no influential representatives in the centers of power, and I find it difficult to believe that literature can change it. But it can offer different ways to live in it. To live with an internal rhythm and an internal continuity that fulfill our emotional and spiritual needs far more than what is violently imposed upon us by the external systems.

I know that when I read a good book, I experience internal clarification: my sense of uniqueness as a person grows lucid. The measured, precise voice that reaches me from the outside animates voices within me, some of which may have been mute until this other voice, or this particular book, came and woke them. And even if thousands of people are reading the very same book I am reading at the very same moment, each of us faces it alone. For each of us, the book is a completely different kind of litmus test.

A good book—and there are not many, because literature too, of course, is subject to the seductions and obstacles of mass media—individualizes and extracts the single reader out of the masses. It gives him an opportunity to feel how spiritual contents, memories, and existential possibilities can float up and rise from within him, from unfamiliar places, and they are his alone. The fruits of his personality alone. The result of his most intimate refinements. And in the mass culture of daily life, in the overall pollution of our consciousness, it is so difficult for these soulful contents to emerge from the inner depths and be animated.

At its best, literature can bring us together with the fate of those who are distant and foreign. It can create within us, at times, a sense of wonder at having managed, by the skin of our teeth, to escape those strangers' fates, or make us feel sad for not being truly close to them. For not being able to reach out and touch them. I am not saying that this feeling immediately motivates us to any form of action, but certainly without it no act of empathy or commitment or responsibility can be possible.

At its best, literature can be kind to us: it can slightly

allay our sense of insult at the dehumanization that results from living in large, anonymous global societies.
The insult of describing ourselves in coarse language,
in clichés, in generalizations and stereotypes. The insult of our becoming—as Herbert Marcuse said—
"one-dimensional man."

Literature also gives us the feeling that there is a way
to fight the cruel arbitrariness that decrees our fate: even
if at the end of *The Trial* the authorities shoot Joseph K.
"like a dog"; even if Antigone is executed; even if Hans
Castorp eventually dies in *The Magic Mountain*—still
we, who have seen them through their struggles, have
discovered the power of the individual to be human
even in the harshest circumstances. Reading—literature—
restores our dignity and our primal faces, our human
faces, the ones that existed before they were blurred and
erased among the masses. Before we were expropriated,
nationalized, and sold wholesale to the lowest bidder.

———

When I finished writing *See Under: Love*, I realized that
I had written it to say that he who destroys a man, any
man, is ultimately destroying a creation that is unique
and boundless, that can never again be reconstructed,
and there will never be another like it.

For the last four years I have been writing a novel
that wishes to say the same thing, but from a different
place, and in the context of a different reality. The protagonist of my book, an Israeli woman of about fifty, is
the mother of a young soldier who goes to war. She fears

for his life, she senses catastrophe lurking, and she tries with all her strength to fight the destiny that awaits him. This woman makes a long and arduous journey by foot, over half the land of Israel, and talks about her son. This is her way of protecting him. This is the only thing she can do now, to make his existence more alive and solid: *to tell the story of his life.*

In the little notebook she takes on her journey, she writes, *Thousands of moments and hours and days, millions of deeds, endless acts and attempts and mistakes and words and thoughts, all to make one person in the world.*

Then she adds another line: *One person, who is so easy to destroy.*

———

This evening, at the opening of the International Literature Festival Berlin, we are allowed to remind ourselves, even with a modicum of pride, that the secret allure and the greatness of literature, which we will dwell upon during these days, the secret that sends us to it over and over again, with enthusiasm and a longing to find refuge and meaning—the secret is that literature can repeatedly redeem for us the tragedy of the one from the statistics of the millions. The one about whom the story is written, and the one who reads the story.

International Literature Festival Berlin, September 4, 2007

Contemplations on Peace

Peace between Israel and the Palestinians, and between Israel and the entire Arab world, is unfortunately still a matter for hopes, speculations, and conjectures. In recent years it seems only to be growing more distant. But even now—and perhaps now all the more vigorously—we must constantly think about the image of this remote peace, and regularly "massage" the way we envision it.

Since the collapse of the Oslo peace process, roughly a decade ago, only a few have had the emotional strength to extract themselves from the hell of daily life, on the streets of Israel and Palestine, and to remember that there is even a possibility for a different life, a life of peace between these rigid enemies. If we do not remind ourselves of the possible faces of peace, if we do not continuously endeavor to imagine it as a realistic option, as an alternative to the existing condition, we will remain with nothing but the desperation caused by war and occupation and terror—the desperation that *causes* war and occupation and terror.

This evening I would like to discuss one aspect of the possible ramifications of peace between Israel and its neighbors: the question of how such peace may help Israel heal from the wounds and the distortions that currently ail it and hinder its normal development as a state and as a society. Since my time is limited, I will not dwell on certain equally weighty questions, such as the effect of possible peace on the entire Middle East, on the Arab states, and on the Palestinians. Nor will I be able to touch upon a topic that I hold dear to my heart: the future of the relationship between the Jewish majority and the Arab minority within the State of Israel. I will try to focus on issues seldom addressed in the attempts to describe and imagine a future peace.

First, I feel that the very ability and willingness to imagine a state of peace means, primarily, believing that we, the Israelis, have a future. I am not even speaking of a good future or a bad future at this point, but of *the mere possibility of there being a future*. Of a solid faith in the idea that Israel will exist for many years to come, a prospect that is by no means certain in the minds of many Israelis.

Perhaps the root of the almost unconscious affinity between "peace" and "future" in the Hebrew language lies in the fact that the short history of the State of Israel, and the much longer history of the Jewish people, comprises almost no prolonged periods of absolute peace, of being in a state of unthreatened tranquillity and security. And so, in Jewish and Israeli consciousness, the word "peace" is always deeply connected with a wish, a hope, not necessarily an existing, concrete state. The Hebrew word for "peace" (*shalom*) seems to be unique: it is a noun, but hiding within it, like a stowaway, is a verb that is always conjugated in the future tense.

The hope for peace is also a primary element in Jewish prayer and in the biblical prophecies of consolation. Only in the future, and in fact only at the end of days, "nation shall not lift up sword against nation, neither shall they learn war any more," as prophesied by Isaiah. And only at the end of days, David promises Jerusalem, will "peace be within thy walls, and prosperity within thy palaces."

"And I will rejoice in Jerusalem," continues Isaiah, "and the voice of weeping shall be no more heard in her, nor the voice of crying. There shall be no more thence an infant of days, nor an old man, that hath not filled his days; for the youngest shall die a hundred years old." (You can surely imagine how these words echo in the current Israeli reality, in which so many parents bury their children, "the youngest.") There is hope and beauty in this affinity between "peace" and "the end of days," yet because the end of days is usually perceived in Jewish-Israeli consciousness as an abstract, utopian, even unattainable point in time, peace too is seen as abstract, utopian, and unattainable: a horizon that grows ever more distant as one approaches it.

When we allow ourselves to seriously contemplate the hope that we will have peace, this inherently contains the possibility that we will have *a future*. A future as a people, a future as a state. This is no trivial matter. For most Israelis the possibility of a future cannot be taken for granted. I do not believe there are many other nations with such a skeptical view of the likelihood that they will indeed have a future, and continuity, and an ongoing existence in the place where they live. When we read in an American newspaper, for example, that the United States is planning its wheat crops for 2025, it sounds completely rational and natural. But what Israeli would dare to speak nonchalantly about the forecast milk production from cows in Israel twenty-one years from now? I myself can attest that when I think about Israel in such future-tense terms, I immediately feel a pang of guilt, as if I had violated some taboo—as if I had allowed myself too large a dose of future.

It is interesting to note that although the Jewish people is so ancient, with such continuity of historical consciousness and identity, it seems that a significant element in its self-definition is the sense of impending annihilation, of the calamity hovering over its head. This is the feeling to which every Jew gives voice at Passover, when he reads in the Haggadah: "That in every generation they rise up to destroy us." This feeling did not, of course, arise out of paranoid delusions, but due to verified historical reasons. But the question that interests us today is whether life in a continued state of peace and existential security might ever alter this feeling, this bitter worldview so deeply ingrained in the Jewish soul, this self-perception that essentially dictates a conditional, fragile existence, a rare state of being among other nations.

Another question follows the previous one, grasping at its heels: What is it like to live without an enemy?

I imagine that to some, particularly those born after the Second World War, this may seem a peculiar query. But like any Israeli, I myself have never known a life without an enemy. I do not know what it means to live my life without the constant presence of an existential threat. Without the urge to fortify ourselves, to protect ourselves, and to act aggressively against those who threaten our homes and sometimes our lives.

I imagine that even if a peace agreement were reached soon, it would be—at least during the first years—fragile and extremely weak, and paved with acts of terror and violence on both sides. We will therefore not have to face the "problem" of living without an enemy anytime soon. But I hope that future generations will have to contend with it.

It will be a huge challenge: to learn to live a life that is not defined by hostility, anxiety, and violence. To foresee a continuum of existence and a constant future. To educate children based on views and beliefs that are not shaped inevitably by the fear of death. To raise our children not based on the daily fear that they may be taken from us at any moment. Perhaps then we may slowly discover that together with the forgoing of anxieties, we can begin to forgo certain elements of the Israeli ethos, a large part of which was forged through military conflict. We may forgo the perception of power as a value in and of itself, and the excessive admiration of power and its agents—the army and the military commanders—an admiration that results in the recurrent election of glorified militarists to lead the country, thereby sentencing it to act according to a narrow military frame of mind, and essentially within a never-ending war.

(In other words: It is highly rational for a nation always in a state of war to elect combatants as its leaders. But could it be possible that the fact that these combatants are the nation's leaders decrees that the nation be in a constant state of war?)

Perhaps, if we know a life of peace, we may also let go of the obsessive need, shared by so many of us, for some artificial "unity," which is viewed as sacred and is supposedly meant to strengthen our standing against anything that may undermine our stability as a society and as a people. Except that in a state of existential anxiety like the one we live in, even a new *challenge*, a new chance, a new hope, is often perceived as a threat to stability, even if that stability is a fairly dismal one; consider, for example, the panicked refusal with which Israel reacts to the repeated signals of peace coming recently from Syria.

The sense of besiegement and the fear of what is being plotted against us beyond the borders inevitably create an eagerness for internal consensus at any cost—a consensus that sometimes seems like the frightened convergence instinct of a threatened herd of cattle. But if the day comes when we do not have to define ourselves in terms of war and besiegement, if we allow ourselves to gradually let go of rigid, narrow-minded, and one-dimensional definitions of those who are "with us" and those who are "against us," of those who are one of "us" and those who are foreigners (and as such, suspected as enemies), perhaps we will slowly learn to be more tolerant of diverse opinions and different voices in politics, art, gender roles, relations between men and women, and, not least, the tense and volatile relationship between Arabs and Jews *within* the State of Israel.

If we ever achieve a state in which we have no enemies, perhaps we will be able to break free from the all-too-familiar Israeli tendency to approach reality with the mind-set of a sworn survivor, who is practically programmed—*condemned*—to define the situations he encounters primarily in terms of threat, danger, and entrapment, or a daring rescue from all these. The survivor ignores anything that may complicate his worldview or delay his reactions, and so he tends to ignore the gray areas, the nuances, without truly facing the complex and contradictory nature of reality, with all the chances and promises it offers. He thereby all but dooms himself to exist forever within this partial, distorted, suspicious, and frightened picture of reality, and is therefore tragically fated to make his anxieties and nightmares come true time and time again.

Will we finally be able to break free from the paralyzing existential paradox of the Jewish people, a people that throughout its entire history has *survived in order to live*, and now finds itself, at least in Israel, *living in order to survive* and not much more? These aggressive, survivor-like tendencies are working their ill effect within Israeli society. It seems that after more than a century of cease-less military and political struggles, of wars and combat operations, of self-defense and endless cycles of revenge and retaliation, the suspicion and hostility with which Is-raelis have become accustomed to viewing the Other, the enemy, have become almost habitual ways of thinking and acting toward *any other*, even if he is "one of the family," even if he is a *brother*.

How little understanding and sympathy we Israelis have toward other Israelis who do not belong to our "group" or "tribe." With what fury or belittlement we treat the real, authentic pain felt by Israelis who are not "us." As if our continual and automatic refusal to recog-nize, even ever so slightly, the suffering of the Palestini-ans, lest this detract from our justness in some way, has now completely disrupted our common sense and our natural familial instinct. Thus, gradually, the sense of affinity and solidarity felt by many Israelis with other groups in our society has waned. Thus a deep hostility is developing between secular and religious; between new immigrants, older immigrants, and native Israelis; be-tween rich and poor; between Jewish Israelis and Arab Israelis. Thus the social and civic cohesion and the per-sonal identification with the state and its goals are wavering. Thus the very fundamental Jewish value of mutual responsibility is eroding. Thus Israelis are gradually losing one of the most important assets of a people—the sense of national identity itself.

———

I shall say a few words about security. I am not an expert, and security professionals may dismiss my thoughts as the speculations of an amateur. Still, I will try to talk about the things that even a layman like myself can understand.

Security means more than just having a strong military force. In its broader sense, security also means a strong and stable economy; fewer social gaps and greater domestic unity; good education; a strong rule of law; the identification of disparate social groups with the state and its objectives; the commitment of elites to remaining in Israel and contributing their skills for its benefit; and more.

Today, Israel has a commanding army, which is a good thing. The Middle East is still a violent and volatile neighborhood. Even if it achieves peace, Israel will always have to be on guard and be prepared for surprises. Israel's army is becoming increasingly fatigued, partly in the moral sense, since a significant proportion of its operations are carried out against civilians, including women and children, in the occupied Palestinian territories. But the army is still able to perform its role of defending the country. Most of the state's other security

components, however, are lacking: four years after the
outbreak of the intifada, the Israeli economy is in a re-
cession unlike any since the 1950s. The cost incurred by
Israel in these four years is estimated at roughly ninety
billion shekels. Poverty, hunger, unemployment, and
crime are growing at an alarming rate, attesting to the
depletion of the welfare and aid systems and the dam-
aged status of the rule of law. The income disparity between the upper and the lower percentiles in Israel is
one of the highest in the world. The worse the security
situation gets, the larger the weight of security expendi-
tures becomes, and the government's power to reduce
social gaps decreases. For the first time in Israel, there
have been public warnings against a widespread violent
social uprising.

But the cracks in the sense of security are deeper and
more fundamental: in recent years, the years of the second intifada, Israelis have been living in a world in which
people are, quite literally, being ripped apart. Entire
families are killed in the blink of an eye, human limbs
severed in cafés, shopping malls, and buses. These are
the materials of Israeli reality and the nightmares of
every Israeli, and the two are inseparably mingled. Much
of daily life in Israel now occurs in the pre-cultural, prim-
itive, animalistic regions of terror. Fierce violence is em-
ployed against the Israelis, and they respond with equal
ruthlessness against the Palestinians. To be an Israeli today means to live with the perception that we have lost
our path and that we are living in a dismantled state, in

every sense—the dismantling of the private, human body, whose fragility is exposed over and over again, and the dismantling of the public, general body. Deep fault lines have emerged in recent years in the various branches of government, in the authority of law and of the courts, in the credibility of the army and the police, and in the trust that the public affords its leaders and its faith in their integrity.

A survey conducted over the last Jewish New Year found that the majority of the public does not believe Israel can ensure its younger generation a better future. Approximately one-quarter of the respondents said they were seriously considering emigration. Hundreds of Israelis gather at the Polish embassy in Tel Aviv every week to obtain Polish citizenship. (Think of the terrible irony—Poland!) They want foreign passports so that it will be easier for themselves and their children to move to European Union countries, possibly for work reasons but also, certainly, to hold on to an option of refuge and escape from Israel.

Because even after fifty-six years of independent sovereignty, still the earth trembles beneath Israelis' feet. Israel has not yet managed to establish among its citizens the sense that this place is their home. They may feel that Israel is their fortress, but still not truly their *home*. The State of Israel has failed to assuage in the hearts of many of its citizens the urge—so Jewish, so human and understandable—to constantly examine alternate ways of existing and possible places of refuge.

Of course the responsibility for this condition cannot be placed solely on Israel under any circumstances. Israeli fears are not merely the result of delusions or the fruit of Israeli mistakes alone. The Middle East has never internalized Israel as an integral component, as a state that exists there by right, not by grace. The Arab states have never demonstrated tolerance or understanding of Israel's unique situation and the unique fate of the Jewish people, and they should not be absolved of responsibility for the tragedy of the Middle East. It is no wonder, then, that Israelis' feeling of being at home among their neighbors, in their historical homeland, is deficient.

The lyrics of a popular Israeli song lament, "I have no other country," and many Israelis do feel this way. Yet it seems that after almost six decades, Israelis overwhelmingly feel that they are not truly living in their own natural home, where they can be safe and unquestioned. Rather, they are still people inhabiting a territory fiercely contested by their neighbors, who may indeed have certain rights to it. Their place is still a disputed area, and not infrequently a disaster zone. It is a territory that perhaps one day, in the unforeseeable future, will become a real home and provide them with everything a home should give its dwellers.

Imagine how difficult such a feeling is. The primary purpose of Zionism—to say nothing of the religious and spiritual aspirations to Zion during the centuries preceding political Zionism—was that Jews could return *home* to create one place in the world where the Jewish individual and the Jewish nation would truly feel at home. It was to be a place where they would not be treated as guests or as strangers to be tolerated, and not as parasites, but as the inhabitants and the landlords of their home. And at this state of tranquillity and security we have not yet arrived.

I do not mean to minimize all the enormous accomplishments Israel has made. Despite an almost impossible starting point, and while fighting an endless war for existence, Israel has created a democratic regime, absorbed millions of immigrants, developed a culture, renewed a language, produced some of the most advanced agriculture in the world, established one of the strongest militaries in the world (and in a world of war, and in light of the fact that throughout most of history the Jewish people had no defense force, even a military is a source of pride), and become a leader in information technology. In short, a country with huge achievements, and more than that—huge potential, which has not yet been fully realized, partly because of the reasons I am discussing here today.

To elaborate further on the question of feeling *at home*, I believe that Israelis' confidence in the definition of "home," and in fact in the definition of their own national identity as Israelis, will be far greater after withdrawing from the Occupied Territories and separating from the occupied Palestinian people. I would like to clarify that I do not view the Occupation as the main reason for the Arab states' hostility toward Israel. This hostility existed before the 1967 war, when the territories that are the subject of the conflict today were occupied, and even if the Occupation ends, I do not believe the conflict will be over quickly. But ending the Occupation may begin to unravel this knot of hostility and gradually diminish the flames of historical, national, and religious enmity toward Israel, consequently disentangling some of the imbroglios within Israeli society.

I think the severe rift in Israeli society today results partly from the fact that in the minds of most Jews in Israel, the Occupied Territories do not correspond, intellectually or emotionally, to the borders of Israeli identity. Certainly these territories are part of a religious Jew's identity because they were included in God's promise to Abraham. The Cave of Machpelah, where the biblical forefathers are buried, is in Hebron; Rachel's tomb is in Bethlehem; the Ark of the Covenant was in Shiloh; and on the fields of Bethlehem, Joseph tended his father Jacob's flock. Still it seems that the "flare" of Israeli identity, and of the authentic sense of *home*, for most Israelis, reaches *as far as the Green Line and not beyond it.* There is straightforward evidence of this: The governments of Israel have showered hundreds of millions of dollars on settlements and settlers in the past decades. What is known as the "settlement enterprise" is the largest and most wasteful national project Israel has undertaken since its inception. A massive mechanism of propaganda, enticement, and persuasion—ideological,

religious, and national—was launched by all the governments of Israel, left and right, to impel Israelis to move
to the Occupied Territories en masse. Scandalously excessive financial incentives were offered. But still, after
almost forty years, fewer than 250,000 Israelis live in the
settlements, and the vast majority of them are children
who were born there. In other words, the settler popu-
lation is approximately the size of one midsize city in
Israel.

Surveys and polls taken regularly over the last eleven
years, since the Oslo accords, show that some 70 percent
of Israelis accept the need to partition the country into
two states. They may not be enthusiastic about it, but
they understand that there is no other choice. Moreover,
every reasonable Israeli understands that the approval of
Ariel Sharon's "disengagement" plan in the Knesset last
October was tantamount to the right wing's admitting the
failure of their ideology, which held that it was possible
to control all areas of the biblical "Land of Israel." And
so I say once again that the "flare" of Israeli identity today, among the majority of Israelis, reaches as far as the
Green Line and no farther. Beyond this line, the nature
of the blaze changes: it either cools and melts away indifferently, alienated from what is occurring there, or becomes an exaggerated frenzy, among the settlers and the
various messianic Jews.

In other words, an absurd and destructive state has
emerged whereby a vast share of Israel's national energies, financial and emotional and human assets, and po-

litical and national enthusiasm have been invested by the state's official bodies, for almost four decades, in a territory that most Israelis do not feel belongs to them in any full, natural, or harmonious sense.

I would like to hope that relinquishing the Territories and ending the Occupation, with all these entail, will restore most Israelis to the authentic emotions of their identity. Then, for the first time in years, perhaps since the beginning of political Zionism, since the various borders were drawn for the soon-to-be state and then for the State of Israel, there will be an overlap between the geographical borders and the borders of identity.

This feeling is extremely elusive, and perhaps I find it difficult to put into words because it is one I have never experienced and can only dream of. It is the way a nation can feel itself, feel its identity, like a healthy body that maintains an emotional, "neural" connection to all its parts, all its areas, all its borders, after being released from the difficult conflicts, the dilemmas, and the struggles that related to its different limbs and organs, struggles that made its life such a misery that they threatened its very existence.

There is also the immense relief we will feel once we are released from the state of occupation itself. I believe that even most of the Israelis who wish to control "Greater Israel" do not want to be *occupiers*. They want the land, but they do not want the *state of occupation,* certainly not the contact with the occupied people, which arouses in any normal person—even one with ex-

treme opinions—a sense of injustice and guilt. I have no
doubt that most Israelis, even if their political views align
them with the center or right, are aware of the moral
dilemmas posed by the Occupation. Even if they justify
the Occupation with sophisticated arguments, even if
they efficiently sweep it under the rug of their awareness, they still feel the unease of the moral dilemma.
They live in a continued state of conflict, not only with
their enemy but also with themselves and their own
values.

Because somewhere deep inside, every person knows
when he is committing or colluding with an injustice.
Somewhere deep in the heart of any "reasonable person"
of sound mind, there is a place where he cannot delude
himself regarding his acts and their implications. The
burden created by the injustice—even if it is re-
pressed—is there, and it has effects and it has a price.
And what a relief, what a feeling of repair—of *tikkun*, in
its deepest spiritual sense—there must be in a release
from the state of occupation and from the open and hidden conflicts it engenders.

Perhaps it is pertinent to recall some of the disrup-
tions not often mentioned when discussing the price Israel pays in its current state of occupation, with no peace
and no hope for peace. There is a huge sense of missed
opportunity, which is becoming increasingly widespread
among those for whom Israel was a dream, those who
had hoped to build a moral and just society, a society
with a humanistic, spiritual vision, a society that would

manage to integrate modern life with the ethics of the prophets and the finest Jewish values. I should also mention the disappointment with the fact that we, the Jews, who have always regarded power with suspicion, have become intoxicated with power ever since it was given us. Intoxicated with power and with authority, and afflicted with all the diseases that limitless power has brought to nations far stronger and more stable than Israel. Unlimited power brings unlimited authority and a virtually unhindered temptation to hurt the helpless, to exploit them economically, to humiliate them culturally, and to scorn them personally.

I must also talk of the price of life without hope. Of the rise of a fatalistic, defeatist frame of mind that has caused many Israelis to feel that the situation will never improve, that *the sword shall devour forever,* and that there is some sort of "divine decree" that dooms us to kill and be killed for eternity. Fifty or sixty years ago, the new Jewish settlement movement (the *yishuv*) in young Israel was prepared to make any sacrifice, because it felt that its purpose was singularly just. Whereas now, for significant components in Israel, the purpose no longer seems just; at times, it is not even clear what the purpose *is*. This lack of meaning, this lack of faith in our leadership and its ways, slowly gnaws at the heart of the matter: at the faith in the just existence of the State of Israel. This internal loss of faith strengthens the view, among certain circles, that the entire State of Israel—not only the settlements—is an act of colonial, capitalist injustice, carried out by an apartheid regime, detached from historical, national, and cultural motives, and therefore illegitimate.

Ending the Occupation could begin to heal some of these internal wounds. I do not believe that a decisive change will happen quickly, but even if it occurs in a generation or two, it can start to bring Israel back from the digressions it has taken from its own ethos. If this happens, there may also emerge a new possibility for the creation of a fascinating synthesis between two fundamental models of the Jewish people: on the one hand, the Jewish Israeli living in his own land, embedded in the earth and the landscapes, the rooted man whose daily reality encompasses all the contradictory layers of reality; and on the other hand, the universal, cosmopolitan Jew who aspires to fulfill a spiritual, moral mission, to be "a light unto the nations," to be the voice of the weak and the oppressed everywhere, to represent a clear, firm value system that derives its strength from ideas, from contemplation, from ethical commitment, who sees in every person a great creation, unique and unrepeated, in the spirit of Isaiah's prophecy and the prophecies of modern thinkers such as Franz Rosenzweig, Martin Buber, and George Steiner.

Think for a moment of the possible merging of these two models! Think of an Israel that manages to create for itself a new, unique place in the family of nations, becoming a self-confident sovereign state whose identity, heritage, and power derive from a universal human com-

mitment, participation in the troubles of the world, and
an insistence on taking a moral stand on questions of society, policy, and economics—an Israel that offers hu-
manitarian aid anywhere it is needed. In other words, a
State of Israel that fulfills the Jewish people's historical
and moral destiny within human history.

Sometimes a thought steals into one's heart: What
would have happened had Israel been able to emerge
and live on as a unique national creation rather than,
with remarkable speed, turn into a clumsy and awkward
imitation of Western countries? What would have happened if Israel had made a national and social choice far
more daring and far-reaching than the one in which it is
currently stagnating? A choice that combined what is often called "the Jewish genius" with the loftiest universal
and Jewish ideals, together with a humane economic and
social system that centers on people and not on capital
and competitiveness; a choice that had some unique,
even genius spark—as did, for example, the kibbutz idea
at its inception, before it eroded and crumbled, and as
did the contributions of Judaism to many varied areas of
human existence, in science and economics, in art and
moral philosophy.

I know that these ideas sound utopian, perhaps
even naive. But there is a shred of utopian thought and
wishful thinking in everything I have said. It is certainly
possible that part of my own private healing process—
perhaps not only my own—from the almost-chronic disease of the "situation" is to once again believe that it is

possible to escape from the shackling, desperate day-to-day, from the great mistake that looms over our every step and gradually stifles our souls, from the cynicism that tramples every hope.

I must also admit that I am a great believer in "acquired naïveté," by which I mean a conscious and determined decision to be somewhat naive, precisely in a situation that is all but rotting away with sobriety and cynicism, that for years has been leading us astray. It is a naïveté that knows full well what it faces and what it contends with, but it also knows that despair creates more despair, hatred, and violence, while hope—even if it is the product of this "acquired naïveté"—may very slowly bring about the mechanisms of prospect, of faith in the possibility of change, of extricating oneself from an eternal victim mentality.

———

I have mentioned the sense of identity, and of being at home, which Israelis might derive from a peace agreement. But one cannot talk of a home without mentioning its walls, the *borders*. In the fifty-six years of Israel's existence, there has not been a single decade during which the country had permanent and stable borders. In 1947 an international border was established, and immediately moved as a result of the 1948 war. In 1956 the southern border was altered following the war with Egypt and the occupation of the Sinai Peninsula, and its subsequent evacuation. The Six-Day War in 1967 expanded Israel's

area fivefold, unrecognizably altering its borders to the
north, east, and south. The war of 1973 and peace with
Egypt in 1977 once again redrew Israel's borders, sever-
ing it from the Sinai Peninsula. The 1982 Lebanon War
brought the Israeli army deep into Lebanese territory,
and essentially pushed the border a few dozen kilome-
ters to the north for eighteen years. The Oslo accords in
1993, and peace with Jordan in 1994, changed Israel's
eastern border with Jordan and the Palestinian Authority. This eastern border is utterly breached, illusory even,
because of the massive presence of settlements in the
heart of the Palestinian areas.

Incidentally, the only border that Israelis find instinctively clear and concrete is their western one—the sea. If
I were to say this in Israel, everyone would nod under-
standingly, although the notion may not be very politically correct. (It is interesting that the sea, the most
unstable, fluid, and deceptive natural element, is the one
that in our perception is the *only* stable border.)

The citizens of Israel have no clear concept of a border. Living this way means living in a home where all the
walls are constantly moving and open to invasion. A person whose home has no solid walls finds it very difficult
to know where it "ends" and where the next home "begins." The result of this ambiguity is that such a person's identity is always on the defense, always "contra" to
those who threaten him. This condition provokes in his
neighbors a constant temptation to invade, and his own
behavior is characterized by a tendency to be overly

defensive—meaning aggressive. The choices he makes in moments of distress or doubt are virtually doomed to be hasty and belligerent. The lessons he is capable of learning from his own history are bound to be the most extreme, and therefore often the most simplistic, the least nuanced—lessons that often damage his perception of reality.

In a certain sense, the State of Israel is replaying one of the most problematic anomalies of the Jewish people in the Diaspora, and the root of its tragic existence over the past two thousand years: it is a nation living among other nations, most of whom are hostile, with no clearly defined borders. This means that every contact may be experienced, by both parties, as a dangerous infiltration into sensitive, loaded identity regions.

I dream of a time when the State of Israel finally has permanent, stable, defensible borders, recognized by the UN and by the entire world, including the Arab states, the United States, and Europe. Borders that will be negotiated with former enemies out of mutual agreement, rather than drawn unilaterally and coercively—as Israel is doing today with the wall it is building around itself. The meaning of the new borders will be security. It will be identity. It will be home.

The meaning of such borders will also be that the Jewish people can finally resolve the critical dilemma of its entire existence: the question of whether it is a "nation of place" or a "nation of time." Are the Jewish people a "nation of eternity," a "nation of the world," unconnected and uncommitted to any one physical place, able to exist within the universal sphere of religion and culture and spirituality alone? Or is it now ripe to begin a new stage, a stage that will be the true and complete realization of the process begun in 1948, when the State of Israel was established?

In other words, an agreement on the borders of Israel, and a normalization of relations with all its neighbors, will gradually be able to answer the extremely complex and loaded question of whether the Jews are truly willing *and able* to live in a state with permanent, unambiguous borders, to live with a clear *national* definition. Or are they instead doomed—because of reasons I will not go into, and which are possibly more emotional than political—to continue their search for a "borderless" existence, in its deepest sense, for a state of constant motion, of intermittent exile and return, assimilation in other identities, and subsequent returns to Jewish identity? Such a condition persistently evades definition, impenetrable to all forces acting around it, forces that sometimes enrich and fertilize it, and sometimes, as has often occurred, try to annihilate it.

One can also hope that a peace agreement resulting in safe and stable borders will heal a deep deficiency in Israelis' sense of acceptance into the political, international "normalcy" that has eluded them for hundreds of years, even though they have had their own state for much of that time. Because this, perhaps, is the greatest tragedy of the Jewish people: that throughout its history it has always been viewed by other peoples and religions, primarily Christianity and Islam, *as a symbol or a metaphor* for something else—a parable, a religious moral of retribution for a primordial sin. It has not been seen as "the thing itself," as a nation among nations, as a person among persons.

For almost two thousand years, the Jew was distanced and exiled from the practical political reality of what is known as "the family of nations." His humanity was denied through a variety of sophisticated means of dehumanization and, conversely, idealization—and these are two sides of the same coin. He was laden with fears and superstitions, treated as an anomalous, mysterious, metaphysical entity with an internal order that is different from others, and with hidden powers that are above nature—and sometimes beneath it, as the Nazis proclaimed when they defined the Jew as *Untermensch*.

Judas Iscariot, God killer, Antichrist, the Wandering Jew, the Eternal Jew, well-poisoners, spreaders of plagues, the Elders of Zion seeking world domination, and many other satanic and grotesque characters, Shylocks and Fagins, have trickled into folklore, religion, literature, and even science. Perhaps this is why the Jews found comfort in self-idealization, in viewing themselves as the chosen people, which is also, in and of itself, a problematic and obstructive perception, and one all the more isolating.

I am alluding here to a subtle and extremely delicate sense, a sense of profound foreignness in the world. An existential foreignness of the Jewish people among others. An existential loneliness that perhaps can only be understood by Jews. An aura of riddle and mystery that has encompassed the Jewish nation—and Jewish people—over the generations. A riddle that has spurred other nations to solve it in various ways, to ascribe racial and racist definitions to the Jews, to repeatedly delineate them with fences and ghettos, to restrict their living space, their professions, their rights, all culminating in the most definitive and terrible attempt to "solve" this Jewish riddle: the "final solution."

If we look back a mere decade, to the days of the early Oslo process, we can recall what an important change occurred at that time in the worldview, and in the self-perception, of Israelis. In those days many Israelis began to taste the intoxicating flavor of a new way of belonging to the modern world, an acceptance of sorts into a progressive, civic, liberal, and essentially secular universalism. It seemed as though some sort of nation-among-nations normalcy was emerging. For a short while, very short, there was a chance to create a relationship that would be more mutual, more equal, less loaded, between Israel and "the rest of the world." I will even dare to employ a somewhat "literary" or metaphorical description: there was a sense of *acceptance into reality.*

And then, over the past four years—as a result of the severe threat created by the intifada and the terrorist attacks, the overwhelming hostility around the world to Israel's acts and at times to its very existence, the swell of anti-Semitism, and the increasing demonization of Israel—these same Israelis found themselves once again sucked into the tragic wound of Judaism, into the scars of its most painful and paralyzing memories. Israeliness itself, which was always directed at the future, comprising constant agitation and promise, seemed to shrink and seep back into the channels of trauma and pain that pervade Jewish history and memory. The result is that among "new" Israelis, the anxieties of the Jewish fate, the experience of persecution and victimhood, the sense of profound loneliness and existential alienation, are once again surfacing powerfully.

(In this context, it is interesting to note that Israel is still known, even among its citizens, as "the Promised Land." Not "the land that was promised" or "the land of promise," but, ostensibly, the land that is still in a permanent state of being "promised." Even after the "return of Zion" and the establishment of a sovereign state, Israel is still perceived by its residents as not entirely realized, and certainly not having fulfilled all its potential. In a state of "eternal promise" there is of course the hope for momentum and the potential for great liberty—liberty of thought and creation, and a flexibility of viewpoints on things that have become set in their definitions. But this state is also afflicted by a curse of "eternal unfulfillment" that engenders a latent sense of inability to ever achieve full realization and full contact with all aspects of reality, and therefore an incapacity to normalize the fundamental questions of identity, of place, of clear borders, and of neighborly relations.)

Could real peace begin the Israeli-Jewish process of
healing from those distresses and anomalies? Moreover,
will "the world"—namely, the Christian and Muslim
worlds, as well as regions dominated by other faiths
and religions, and states where anti-Semitism prevails,
whether openly or as an undercurrent—be able to heal
itself of its distorted approach to Israel and to Judaism?
Will it ever be able to let go of its racism toward Jews?
With your permission, I will leave these momentous
questions open. I do not have the answers.

———

There is one more unanswered question: What will really
happen to Israeli society, now polarized and conflict-
ridden, if the external threat is removed—the threat that
currently protects it from internal strife and "helps" it
avoid confronting the contentious issues? To an outside
observer this may seem an unfounded and even fantasti-
cal question, but it has been hovering in Israeli public
space for decades, so much so that one can sometimes
hear statements along the lines of "The war with the
Arabs saves us from civil war."

I have no doubt that removing the external threat
from Israel will clear a large space for it to cope with
its profound domestic troubles. Although the crux of
the central argument between "right" and "left," on the
question of the Occupation, will be dulled, other issues
will jump to the forefront: the vast social and economic
gaps, the tense relations between secular and religious

Jews, between Jews and Arabs, and between different immigrant groups who are unable and unwilling to understand one another. Such circumstances may expose the fragility of the diverse and diffuse immigrant society that has emerged in Israel. They may also reveal the weakness of the democratic worldview, which does not seem to have been truly internalized by most citizens, both because they came to Israel from countries that never knew democracy and because it is impossible for a state to maintain true democracy while simultaneously upholding a regime of occupation and oppression.

Still, only a madman or a complete cynic would prefer Israel's century-old state of war to a state of peace, bad as it may be. Even if internal conflicts do erupt, even if genies are let out of their bottles, they will be *our* genies, the internal, authentic identity materials of the State of Israel and Israeli society. In some sense, the developments that occur then, though they may be painful, will be far more relevant to the construction of Israeli identity than the processes in which Israel has found itself due to the conflict with the Arabs. The fact that such hesitations are openly voiced and contemplated by many Israelis attests to the powerful destruction and degeneration that can result from prolonged exposure to the cancerous rays of war.

———

"Here in the land our ancestors cherished, all our hopes will come true," our pioneering forefathers sang when they came to *Eretz Yisrael* roughly a century ago. Today it is clear that many years will pass before even a fraction of "all our hopes" comes true. It will be very difficult to relinquish the distortions of violence and anxiety, as it is sometimes difficult for a slave to lose his shackles or for someone to let go of a defect around which his entire personality has been constructed.

Because the situation we live in, in Israel, in Palestine, in the Middle East, has become a sort of national and personal defect. Many of us have become so used to the deformation that we find it difficult to even believe in any other existence. Others create entire ideologies, political and religious, to *ensure* the continuation of the present situation.

Hegel said that history is made by evil people. In the Middle East, I think we know that the opposite is also true: we have seen how a certain history can make people evil. We know that prolonged existence in a state of hostility, which leads us to act more stringently, more suspiciously, in a crueler and more "military" manner, slowly kills something within our souls and finally hardens like an internal mask of death over our consciousness, our volition, our language, and our simple, natural happiness.

These are the real dangers that Israel must act quickly to avoid. Israel needs to experience a life of peace, not only because peace is essential for its security and economy, but so that it can, in a sense, *get to know itself.* So that it can discover everything that is still present, though dormant, in its being: the parts of its identity and personality, and the possibilities of existence, that have been suspended until the anger dies down, until the war ends, until it can be allowed to live life to the fullest in all its dimensions, not only the narrow dimension of survival at any cost.

Elias Canetti writes in one of his essays that survival is in fact a repeated experience of death. A sort of practice of death and of the fear of death. At times I feel that a nation of sworn survivors like the Jewish people is a nation that somehow addresses death at least as insistently as it addresses life, a nation whose intimate and permanent interlocutor is death, no less than life itself. And I do not mean to imply a romanticization or idealization of death, or even the idea of being in love with death (akin to the prevailing notions in late-nineteenth-century Germany, for example). Rather, I am speaking of something more profound. Of some firsthand knowledge, a bitter knowledge that is passed through the umbilical cord, a knowledge of the concreteness and the actuality and the daily availability of death. A knowledge of the "unbearable lightness of death," whose saddest expression I ever heard was in an interview with an Israeli couple on the eve of their marriage. They were asked how many children they would like to have, and the sweet young bride immediately answered that they wanted three children, "so that if one is killed, we will still have two."

When I hear Israelis, even very young ones, talk about themselves and about their fears, about not daring to hope for a better future, when I am exposed—in those close to me, and in myself—to the powerful existential anxiety and the influence of the tragic historical Jewish memory, I can often feel, chillingly, the failing left in us by history, the terrible tendency to view life as latent death.

In a life of stable and continued peace, this failing and these anxieties may find some cure. If Israel can live in peace with its neighbors, it will have the opportunity to express all of its abilities and all of its uniqueness. To examine, under normal conditions, what it is capable of as a nation and as a society. To discover whether it is able to forge a spiritual and material reality full of life, creation, inspiration, and humanity. To examine whether its Jewish citizens can extricate themselves from the destructive fatal metaphor framed for them by other nations, who have viewed them as eternal strangers, as borderless nomads among nations—to step out of these definitions and become a nation "of flesh and blood." Not just a symbol or an abstract concept, not a parable or a stereotype, not an ideal or a demon. A nation in its country, a nation whose state is surrounded by internationally recognized and defensible borders. A nation that enjoys not only a sense of security and continuity but also a rare experience of *actuality*, of being, finally, "part of life" and not "larger than life." Perhaps then Israelis will be able to taste what even after fifty-six years of independence they do not truly know—a deep internal sense of security, of "solid existence," like the one expressed so simply and movingly in the *musaf* prayer recited on the Sabbath: "And plant us in our borders."

I conclude with one more wish, which I once expressed in my novel *See Under: Love*. This wish is uttered at the very end of the book, when a group of persecuted Jews in the Warsaw ghetto finds an abandoned baby boy and decides to raise him. These elderly Jews, broken and tortured, stand around the child and dream about what they would like his life to be, and into what sort of a world they would like him to grow up. Behind them, the real world is going up in smoke, with blood and fire everywhere, and they say a prayer together. This is their prayer: "All of us prayed for one thing: that he might end his life knowing nothing of war . . . We asked so little: for a man to live in this world from birth to death and know nothing of war."

Lecture at the Levinas Circle meeting in Paris, December 5, 2004

Yitzhak Rabin Memorial Rally

The annual memorial ceremony for Yitzhak Rabin is the moment when we pause to remember Rabin the man and Rabin the leader. We also look at ourselves, at Israeli society, at its leadership, the national mood, the status of the peace process, and at our own place as private individuals within the national developments. It is not easy to look at ourselves this year.

There was a war. Israel flexed its huge military muscle, revealing nothing but its powerlessness and fragility. We discovered that, ultimately, our military might alone cannot ensure our existence. Moreover, we discovered that Israel is in a profound crisis, far more profound than we had imagined, in almost every aspect of its being.

I am speaking to you this evening as someone whose love for this country is difficult and complicated, but nonetheless unequivocal. And as someone whose long-standing covenant with the country has become, tragically, a covenant of blood. I am a wholly secular man, yet to me the establishment and the very existence of the State of Israel are a sort of miracle that we as a people have experienced—a political, national, human miracle. I do not forget this even for a moment. Even when many things in the reality of our lives outrage and depress me, even as the miracle is broken down into tiny units of routine and misery, of corruption and cynicism, even when reality seems like a bad parody of the miracle, I always remember. And it is from this feeling that I speak to you tonight.

"Behold, earth, for we have been very wasteful," wrote the poet Shaul Tchernichovsky in 1938. He was lamenting the fact that in the earth of Israel, time after time, we bury young people in the prime of their lives.

The death of a young person is a terrible, shattering waste. But no less terrible is the sense that for many years the State of Israel has been criminally wasting not only the lives of its children, but also the miracle it experienced—the great and rare chance bestowed upon it by history, the chance to create an enlightened, decent, democratic state that would conduct itself according to Jewish and universal values. A state that would be a national home and a refuge, but not *only* a refuge: rather, a place that would also give new meaning to Jewish existence. An essential part of the Jewish identity of this state, of its Jewish ethos, was to be a thoroughly egalitarian and respectful attitude toward its non-Jewish citizens.

And look what has happened.

Look what has happened to the young, daring, enthusiastic, and soulful country that used to be here. See how, through some accelerated aging process, Israel has leaped from infancy, through childhood and adolescence, to a permanent state of discontent, weakness, and missed opportunities. How did this happen? When did we lose even the hope that we could ever live a different life, a better life? Moreover, how can we continue to stand by and watch, as if hypnotized, as our home is taken over by madness and coarseness, violence and racism?

And how, I ask you, is it possible that a nation with our powers of creativity and renewal, a nation that has managed to resurrect itself from the ashes time after time, finds itself today—precisely when it has such huge military power—flaccid and helpless? A victim once again—but this time, a victim of itself, of its own anxieties and despair, of its own nearsightedness?

One of the harshest outcomes of the recent war is our heightened sense that there is no king in Israel. That our leadership is hollow. Both the political and the military leadership. I am not speaking of the obvious failures in the way the war was conducted, nor of the neglect of the home front. Nor of the corruption, small and large. I am speaking of the fact that the people who are leading Israel today are incapable of connecting Israelis with their identity—certainly not a healthy, animating, nurturing identity, one comprising the foundations, the memories, and the values that could give Israelis strength and hope.

Such an identity would be an antidote to the waning of mutual responsibility and attachment to the country; it would give meaning to the exhausting and dispiriting struggle for existence.

The main substances with which Israeli leadership fills the shell of its rule today are primarily those of fear, on the one hand, and intimidation, on the other. The enchantment of power, the wink of the quick fix. Wheeling and dealing in all we hold dear. In this respect, they are not true leaders, and they cannot help a nation adrift in such a complicated state of affairs. Sometimes it seems as though the echoes of our leaders' thoughts, of their historical memory, of their vision, of the things they truly care about, exist solely in the tiny space between two newspaper headlines. Or between two investigations by the attorney general.

Look at the people who are leading us. Not all of them, of course, but too many of them. Look at the scared, suspicious, sweaty ways they behave, at their prosecutorial, deceptive conduct. It is ridiculous even to hope that they might be the source of any inspiration, any vision, even so much as an original idea, something truly creative, daring, imaginative. When was the last time the prime minister conceived or implemented a move that had the power to open a single new horizon for Israelis? A better future? When did he initiate a social, cultural, or moral measure, rather than frenetically react to the measures imposed on him by others?

Mr. Prime Minister, I am not saying these things out

of anger or vengefulness. I have waited long enough so that I would not be responding out of any fleeting impulse. You cannot dismiss my words tonight by saying that a man should not be judged at his time of grief. Of course I am in grief. But more than anger, what I feel is pain. I am pained by this country, and by what you and your friends are doing to it. Believe me, your success is important to me, because the future of us all depends on your ability to stand up and do something.

Yitzhak Rabin turned to the path of peace with the Palestinians not because he felt any great affection for them or their leader. Then too, as we recall, the general opinion was that we had no partner among the Palestinians, and that there was nothing to talk about. Rabin decided to do something because he observed, wisely, that Israeli society could not continue to exist for very long in a state of unresolved conflict. He understood before many others did that life in a constant climate of violence, occupation, terror, anxiety, and hopelessness was taking a toll that Israel could not withstand. These things are still true today, even more sharply so. In a moment we shall talk about the partner we do or do not have. First, let us look at ourselves.

For more than a century we have been living in strife. We, the citizens of this conflict, were born into war, schooled in it, and in some ways programmed for it. Perhaps this is why we sometimes think that this madness in which we have been living for over a hundred years is the real thing, the only thing, the only life we were

meant to live, and that we do not have the option, or
even the *right*, to aspire to another life: we shall live by
the sword and we shall die by the sword, and the sword
shall devour forever.

Perhaps this explains the indifference with which we
accept the total failure of the peace process, a failure
that has been going on for years, demanding more and
more victims. This may also explain the general lack of
response to the heavy blow against democracy dealt by
the appointment of Avigdor Lieberman as a senior minister—the appointment of a known pyromaniac to run
the national fire brigade. These are also some of the fac-
tors that have contributed to Israel's remarkably rapid
decline into coldness and real cruelty toward the weak,
the poor, and the suffering. An indifference to the fate of
the hungry, the elderly, the sick, and the handicapped; a
national apathy toward the trade in women, for instance,
or the exploitation and slave conditions of foreign workers; a deep-seated, institutionalized racism toward the
Arab minority. When all these can occur here so naturally, arousing neither shock nor protest, I begin to fear
that even if peace comes tomorrow, even if we ever return to some sort of normality, it may already be too late
for a full recovery.

———

The tragedy that befell my family and me upon the death
of our son Uri does not give me special privileges in the
public discourse. But I believe that facing death and loss

brings a kind of sobriety, a clarity, or at least an enhanced capacity to distinguish between primary and secondary. Between what can be obtained and what cannot. Between reality and fantasy.

Any intelligent person in Israel—and, I will add, in Palestine—knows today exactly where the lines of any possible resolution to the conflict between the two peoples lie. Any intelligent person, on our side or theirs, knows deep in his heart the difference between dreams and heartfelt desires, and what may be obtained at the end of negotiations. Whoever does not know this is already not a partner for dialogue, whether Jewish or Arab, because he is trapped in his hermetic fanaticism.

Let us look for a moment at those who are supposed to be our partners. The Palestinians have chosen Hamas to lead them, and Hamas refuses to negotiate with us or even recognize us. What can be done in this situation? What other steps can we take? Should we keep smothering them? Keep killing hundreds of Palestinians in Gaza, the vast majority of whom are innocent civilians like ourselves?

Go to the Palestinians, Mr. Olmert. Go to them over the head of Hamas. Go to the moderates among them, the ones who, like me and you, oppose Hamas and its ways. Go to the Palestinian people. Speak to their deep wounds, recognize their continued suffering. Your status will not be diminished, nor will that of Israel in any future negotiations. But people's hearts will begin to open a little to one another, and this opening has huge power.

Simple human compassion is as strong as a force of nature, particularly in a state of stagnation and hostility.

For once, look at them not only through the crosshairs of a rifle or a roadblock. You will see a nation no less tortured than we are. A nation occupied and oppressed and hopeless. Of course the Palestinians are also to blame for the dead end. Of course they had a part in the failure of the peace process. But look at them for a moment in a different light. Not only at the extremists among them, those who have an alliance of interests with our own extremists. Look at the overwhelming majority of this miserable people, whose fate is bound up with ours whether we like it or not.

Go to the Palestinians, Mr. Olmert. Do not keep searching for reasons not to talk with them. You gave up on the unilateral "convergence" plan. That was the right thing to do. But do not leave a void, for it will fill up at once with violence and destruction. Talk to them. Give them an offer that the moderates among them can accept (they are more numerous than the media suggest). Give them a proposal, so that they will have to decide whether to accept it or remain hostages of a fanatic Islam. Come to them with the bravest and most serious plan Israel is capable of offering. With the proposal that every reasonable Israeli and Palestinian knows is the limit of refusal and compromise, ours and theirs. If you delay, we will soon be nostalgic for the amateurism of Palestinian terror. We will beat our heads and shout: How did we not employ all our intellectual resilience, all our Israeli creativity, to uproot our enemy from within its own trap?

Just as there is a war of no choice, there is also a peace of no choice. Because there is no choice anymore. We have no choice, and they have no choice. And a peace of no choice should be pursued with the same determination and creativity with which one goes to a war of no choice. Because there is no choice. Whoever thinks there is, or that time is in our favor, does not grasp the dangerous underlying processes that are already occurring.

Furthermore, Mr. Prime Minister, perhaps you need to be reminded that if any Arab leader sends signals of peace, even the slightest and most hesitant ones, you must respond. You must immediately find out whether he is sincere and in earnest. *You do not have the moral right not to respond.* You must do this for the sake of those whose lives you will demand as sacrifice if another war breaks out. If President Assad says Syria wants peace, even if you do not believe him—and we are all suspicious—you must offer to meet with him that very same day. Do not wait even one day. When you went to war, you did not wait so much as one minute. You stormed the battlefield with all your power. With all your weapons. With all your powers of destruction. Why is it that when there is a flicker of peace, you immediately reject it? What do you have to lose? Do you suspect the Syrian president? Go and present him with terms that will expose his plot. Offer him a peace process that will continue for a number of years, after which, if he meets all conditions, all restrictions, he will get the Golan Heights back. Hold him to a process of continued dialogue. Act in such a way that this possibility will emerge in the consciousness of his people. Help the moderates, who surely exist there too. Try to shape reality and not merely be its collaborator. That is what you were elected to do. That—precisely that.

———

In closing, clearly not everything depends on our own actions, and there are stronger forces at work in the region and in the world. Some of them—like Iran, like extreme Islam—seek to harm us. Nevertheless, much depends on what we do and what we are. The disagreements today between right and left are not really that great. The decisive majority of Israeli citizens understand at this point, however reluctantly, what shape the solution to the conflict will take. Most of us understand that the country will be partitioned, that a Palestinian state will arise. Why, then, do we continue to exhaust ourselves with the internal strife that has been going on for almost *forty years*? Why does the political leadership continue to reflect the positions of the extremists and not of the majority? Surely our situation would be far better if we reached a national accord among ourselves before circumstances— external pressures, a new intifada, or another war—force us to do so. If we do that, we will save ourselves from years of decline and mistakes, years in which we will cry out again and again, *Behold, earth, for we have been very wasteful.*

From the place where I stand now, I plead, I call upon anyone who is listening—young people back from war, who know they are the ones who will be asked to pay the price of the next war, Jewish and Arab citizens, right and left: Stop for one moment. Look over the precipice, think how close we are to losing what we have created here. Ask yourselves if the time has not come to pull ourselves back, snap out of the paralysis, and demand for ourselves, finally, the life we deserve to live.

Rabin Square, Tel Aviv, November 4, 2006